The Ragamuffin Gospel

Embracing
the Unconditional
Love of God

The Ragamuffin Gospel

Embracing the Unconditional Love of God

Brennan Manning

To Roslyn, Thank You

Scripture quotations marked JB are from the Jerusalem Bible.

Scripture quotations marked NAB are from the New American Bible.

Cover design by Greg Breeding

Cover illustration by Mike Reed

THE RAGAMUFFIN GOSPEL
© 1990 by Brennan Manning
Published by Multnomah Books
part of the Questar publishing family
Sisters, Oregon 97599

Printed in the United States of America

ISBN 0-88070-631-7

98 99 00 01 02 03 04 05 - 20 19 18 17 16

Contents

Foreword

I owe Brennan Manning thirty dollars for lecture tapes I bought from him on an I.O.U. I'm not writing this foreword because of that debt. I simply mention it because indebtedness is a condition indicative of ragamuffins—a condition we all share, until we lose ourselves in the liberating, healing, invigorating truth to which these pages bear testimony.

My introduction to Brennan Manning's work came on a drive south from Manhattan, Kansas, through the edge of the Flinthills. It is a beautiful drive, best accompanied by the music of Aaron Copeland...or by pure silence. When a friend put a tape of one of Manning's lectures in my truck's tape player, I objected. But my friend said, "Just give it ten minutes."

Five minutes later, I steered the truck onto the shoulder of the road. My eyes were so full of tears, I could not see to drive.

I have attended church regularly since I was less than a week old. I've listened to sermons about virtue, sermons against vice. I have heard about money, time management, tithing, abstinence, and generosity. I've listened to thousands of sermons...but I could count on one hand the number that were a simple proclamation of the gospel of Christ.

That proclamation is the message I heard that day. And it did what the gospel can't help but do: it broke the power of mere "moralistic religiosity" in my life, and revived a deeper acceptance that had long ago withered in me.

In our society, we tend to swear unyielding allegiance to a rigid position, confusing that action with finding an authentic connection to a life-giving Spirit. We miss the gospel of Christ: the good news that, although the holy and all-powerful God knows we are dust, he still stoops to breathe into us the breath of life—to bring to our wounds the balm of acceptance and love. No other author has articulated this message more simply or beautifully than Brennan Manning.

I owe Brennan Manning thirty dollars, and I expect to get it to him soon. But I owe him an even bigger debt for the freedom he helped me find through this book...and the greatest debt of all to the God whose grace extends to—and especially for—the ragamuffins of this world.

Rich Mullins,
songwriter and recording artist
Wichita, Kansas

Acknowledgements

Evelyn Underhill said: "Spiritual reading is, or at least can be, second only to prayer as a developer and support of the inner life." And "The Message of the Wesleys" contains this striking sentence: "It cannot be that people should grow in grace unless they give themselves to reading." Surely a gracious God provides for the illiterate in other ways, but, for most of us, the Scriptures and varied spiritual writings guide us to a deeper understanding of the truth that sets us free.

Humbly and happily, I express my gratitude to several Christian authors upon whom I have relied for deeper insight into Jesus Christ and the Gospel of grace: Edward Schillebeeckx, Walter Burkhardt, Hans Küng, Donald McCullough, Leonard Foley, Eugene Kennedy, Albert Nolan, Jaroslav Pelikan, Sean Caulfield, Anthony de Mello, Lloyd Ogilvie, and others quoted in these pages.

My deepest indebtedness is to my wife, Roslyn, for her honest and candid critique of my work. She never hesitated to tell me when the words were insensitive, misleading, or off-the-wall. I know of no finer tribute of trust in our marriage and mutual love.

Finally, my thanks to John Van Diest and Liz Heaney of Multnomah whose enthusiasm over the first few pages of this book fueled the desire to finish it.

A Word Before

The Ragamuffin Gospel was written with a specific reading audience in mind.

This book is not for the super-spiritual.

It is not for muscular Christians who have made John Wayne and not Jesus their hero.

It is not for academicians who would imprison Jesus in the ivory tower of exegesis.

It is not for noisy, feel-good folks who manipulate Christianity into a naked appeal to emotion.

It is not for hooded mystics who want magic in their religion.

It is not for Alleluia Christians who live only on the mountaintop and have never visited the valley of desolation.

It is not for the fearless and tearless.

It is not for red-hot zealots who boast with the rich young ruler of the gospels: "All these commandments I have kept from my youth."

It is not for the complacent, hoisting over their shoulder a tote-bag of honors, diplomas, and good works actually believing they have it made.

It is not for legalists who would rather surrender control of their souls to rules than run the risk of living in union with Jesus.

If anyone is still reading along, *The Ragamuffin Gospel* was written for the bedraggled, beat-up, and burnt-out.

It is for the sorely burdened who are still shifting the heavy suitcase from one hand to the other.

It is for the wobbly and weak-kneed who know they don't have it altogether and are too proud to accept the handout of amazing grace.

It is for inconsistent, unsteady disciples whose cheese is falling off their cracker.

It is for poor, weak, sinful men and women with hereditary faults and limited talents.

It is for earthen vessels who shuffle along on feet of clay.

It is for the bent and the bruised who feel that their lives are a grave disappointment to God.

It is for smart people who know they are stupid and honest disciples who admit they are scalawags.

The Ragamuffin Gospel is a book I wrote for myself and anyone who has grown weary and discouraged along the Way.

Brennan Manning
New Orleans

Chapter 1

Something is Radically Wrong

On a blustery October night in a church outside Minneapolis, several hundred believers had gathered for a three-day seminar. I began with a one-hour presentation on the gospel of grace and the reality of salvation. Using Scripture, story, symbolism, and personal experience, I focused on the total sufficiency of the redeeming work of Jesus Christ on Calvary. The service ended with a song and a prayer. Leaving the church by a side door, the pastor turned to his associate and fumed.

"Humph, that airhead didn't say one thing about what we have to do to earn our salvation!"

Something is radically wrong.

The bending of the mind by the powers of this world has twisted the gospel of grace into religious bondage and distorted the image of God into an eternal, small-minded bookkeeper. The Christian community resembles a Wall Street exchange of works wherein the elite are honored and the ordinary ignored. Love is stifled, freedom shackled, and self-righteousness fastened. The institutional church has become a wounder of the healers rather than a healer of the wounded.

Put bluntly: the American Church today accepts grace in theory but denies it in practice. We say we believe that the fundamental structure of reality is grace, not works—but our lives refute our faith. By and large, the gospel of grace is neither proclaimed, understood, nor lived. Too many Christians are living in the house of fear and not in the house of love.

Our culture has made the word *grace* impossible to understand. We resonate to slogans such as:

"There's no free lunch."

"You get what you deserve."

"You want money? Work for it."

"You want love? Earn it."

"You want mercy? Show you deserve it."

"Do unto others before they do it unto you."

"Watch out for welfare lines, the shiftless street people, free hot dogs at school, affluent students with federal loans; it's a con game."

"By all means give others what they deserve—but not one penny more."

My editor at Revell told me she overheard a pastor say to a child: "God loves good little boys." As I listen to sermons with their pointed emphasis on personal effort—no pain, no gain—I get the impression that a "do-it-yourself" spirituality is the American fashion.

Though the Scriptures insist on God's initiative in the work of salvation—that by grace we are saved, that the Tremendous Lover has taken to the chase—our spirituality often starts with self, not God. Personal responsibility has replaced personal response. We talk about acquiring virtue as if it were a skill that can be attained like good handwriting or a well-grooved golf swing. In the penitential seasons we focus on overcoming our weaknesses, getting rid of our hang-ups, and reaching Christian maturity. We sweat through various spiritual exercises as if they were designed to produce a Christian Charles Atlas.

Though lip service is paid to the gospel of grace, many Christians live as if it is only personal discipline and self-denial that will mold the perfect me. The emphasis is on what I do rather than on what God is doing. In this curious process God is a benign old spectator in the bleachers who cheers when I show up for morning quiet time. We transfer the Horatio Alger legend of the self-made man into our relationship with God. As we read Psalm 123, "As the eyes of the servant are on the hands of his master, as the eyes of a maid are on the hands of her mistress," we experience a vague sense of existential guilt. Our eyes are not on God. At heart we are practicing Pelagians. We believe that we can pull ourselves up by our bootstraps—indeed, we can do it ourselves.

Sooner or later we are confronted with the painful truth of our inadequacy and insufficiency. Our security is shattered and our bootstraps are cut. Once the fervor has passed, weakness and infidelity appear.

We discover our inability to add even a single inch to our spiritual stature. There begins a long winter of discontent that eventually flowers into gloom, pessimism, and a subtle despair: subtle because it goes unrecognized, unnoticed, and therefore unchallenged. It takes the form of boredom, drudgery. We are overcome by the ordinariness of life, by daily duties done over and over again. We secretly admit that the call of Jesus is too demanding, that surrender to the Spirit is beyond our reach. We start acting like everyone else. Life takes on a joyless, empty quality. We begin to resemble the leading character in Eugene O'Neill's play *The Great God Brown*: "Why am I afraid to dance, I who love music and rhythm and grace and song and laughter? Why am I afraid to live, I who love life and the beauty of flesh and the living colors of the earth and sky and sea? Why am I afraid to love, I who love love?"

Something is radically wrong.

Our huffing and puffing to impress God, our scrambling for brownie points, our thrashing about trying to fix ourselves while hiding our pettiness and wallowing in guilt are nauseating to God and are a flat denial of the gospel of grace.

Our approach to the Christian life is as absurd as the enthusiastic young man who had just received his plumber's license and was taken to see Niagara Falls. He studied it for a minute and then said, "I think I can fix this."[1]

The word itself, *grace*, has become trite and debased through misuse and overuse. It does not move us the way it moved our early Christian ancestors. In some European countries certain high ecclesiastical officials are still called "Your Grace."

Sportswriters speak of Michael Jordan's "easy grace" and entrepreneur Donald Trump has been described as "lacking in grace." A new perfume appears with the label "grace" and a child's report card is called a "disgrace." The word has lost its raw, imaginative power.

Fyodor Dostoyevsky caught the shock and scandal of the gospel of grace when he wrote: "At the last Judgment Christ will say to us, 'Come, you also! Come, drunkards! Come, weaklings! Come, children of shame!' And he will say to us: 'Vile beings, you who are in the image of the beast and bear his mark, but come all the same, you as well.' And the wise and prudent will say, 'Lord, why do you welcome them?' And he will say: 'If I welcome them, you wise men, if I welcome them, you prudent men, it is because not one of them has ever been judged worthy.' And he will stretch out his arms, and we will fall at his feet, and we will cry out sobbing, and then we will understand all, we will understand the Gospel of grace! Lord, your Kingdom come!"[2]

I believe the Reformation actually began the day Martin Luther was praying over the meaning of Paul's words in Romans 1:17. "In the gospel this is what reveals the righteousness of God to us . . . it shows how faith leads to faith, or as Scripture says: the righteous shall find life through faith." Like many Christians today, Luther wrestled through the night with the core question: how could the gospel of Christ be truly called "Good News" if God is a righteous judge rewarding the good and punishing the evil? Did Jesus really have to come to reveal that terrifying message? How could the revelation of God in Christ Jesus be accurately called "news" since the Old Testament carried the same theme, or "good" with the threat of punishment hanging like a dark cloud over the valley of history?

But as Jarislav Pelikan notes, "Luther suddenly broke through to the insight that the 'righteousness of God' that Paul spoke of in this passage was not the righteousness by which God was righteous in himself (that would be passive righteousness,) but the righteousness by which, for the sake of Jesus Christ, God made sinners righteous (that is, active righteousness) through the forgiveness of sins in justification. When he discovered that, Luther said it was as though the very gates of Paradise had been opened to him."[3]

What a stunning truth!

"Justification by grace through faith" is the theologian's learned phrase for what Chesterton once called "the furious love of God." He is not moody or capricious; he knows no seasons of change. He has a single relentless stance toward us: he loves us. He is the only God man has ever heard of who loves sinners. False gods—the gods of human manufacturing—despise sinners, but the Father of Jesus loves all, no matter what they do. But of course this is almost too incredible for us to accept. Nevertheless, the central affirmation of the Reformation stands: through no merit of ours, but by his mercy, we have been restored to a right relationship with God through the life, death, and resurrection of his beloved Son. This is the Good News, the gospel of grace.

With his characteristic *joie de vivre*, Robert Capon puts it this way: "The Reformation was a time when men went blind, staggering drunk because they had discovered, in the dusty basement of late medievalism, a whole cellarful of fifteen-hundred-year-old, two hundred proof grace—of bottle after bottle of pure distillate of Scripture, one sip of which would convince anyone that God saves us single-handedly. The word of the Gospel—after all those centuries of trying to lift yourself into heaven by worrying about the perfection of your bootstraps—suddenly turned out to be a flat announcement that the saved were home before they started. . . . Grace has to be drunk straight: no water, no ice, and certainly no ginger ale; neither goodness, nor badness, nor the flowers that bloom in the spring of super spirituality could be allowed to enter into the case."[4]

Matthew 9:9-13 captures a lovely glimpse of the gospel of grace: "As he moved on, Jesus saw a man named Matthew at his post where taxes were collected. He said to him, 'Follow me.' Matthew got up and followed him. Now it happened that, while Jesus was at table in Matthew's house, many tax collectors and those known as sinners came to join Jesus and his disciples at dinner. The Pharisees saw this and complained to his disciples, 'What reason can the Teacher have for eating with tax collectors and those who disregard the law?' Overhearing their remark, he said, 'People who are in good health do not need a doctor; sick people do. Go and learn the meaning of the words, "It is mercy I desire and not sacrifice." I have come not to call the self-righteous but sinners.' "

Here is revelation bright as the evening star: Jesus comes for sinners, for those as outcast as tax collectors and for those caught up in squalid choices and failed dreams. He comes for corporate executives, street people, superstars, farmers, hookers, addicts, IRS agents, AIDS victims, and even used car salesmen. Jesus not only talks with these people but dines with them—fully aware that his table fellowship with sinners will raise the eyebrows of religious bureaucrats who hold up the robes and insignia of their authority to justify their condemnation of the truth and their rejection of the gospel of grace.

This passage should be read, reread, and memorized. Every Christian generation tries to dim the blinding brightness of its meaning because the gospel seems too good to be true. We think salvation belongs to the proper and pious, to those who stand at a safe distance from the back alleys of existence, clucking their judgments at those who have been soiled by life. In the name of Grace, what has been the verdict of the Christian community on the stained life of the late Rock Hudson? To the disclosure (the $4.5 million settlement to his lover Marc Christian notwithstanding) that he called a priest to his deathbed, confessed his sins, and cried out to God for forgiveness?

Jesus, who forgave the sins of the paralytic (thereby claiming divine power), proclaims that he has invited sinners and not the self-righteous to his table. The Greek verb used here, *kalein*, has the sense of inviting an honored guest to dinner.

In effect, Jesus says the Kingdom of his Father is not a subdivision for the self-righteous nor for those who feel they possess the state secret of their salvation. The Kingdom is not an exclusive, well-trimmed suburb with snobbish rules about who can live there. No, it is for a larger, homelier, less self-conscious cast of people who understand they are sinners because they have experienced the yaw and pitch of moral struggle.

These are the sinner-guests invited by Jesus to closeness with him around the banquet table. It remains a startling story to those who never understand that the men and women who are truly filled with light are those who have gazed deeply into the darkness of their imperfect existence. Perhaps it was after meditating on this passage that Morton Kelsey wrote: "The church is not a museum for saints but a hospital for sinners."

The Good News means we can stop lying to ourselves. The sweet sound of amazing grace saves us from the necessity of self-deception. It keeps us from denying that though Christ was victorious, the battle with lust, greed, and pride still rages within us. As a sinner who has been redeemed, I can acknowledge that I am often unloving, irritable, angry, and resentful with those closest to me. When I go to church I can leave my white hat at home and admit I have failed. God not only loves me as I am, but also knows me as I am. Because of this I don't need to apply spiritual cosmetics to make myself presentable to him. I can accept ownership of my poverty and powerlessness and neediness.

As C.S. Lewis says in *The Four Loves*, "Grace substitutes a full, childlike and delighted acceptance of our need, a joy in total dependence. The good man is sorry for the sins which have increased his need. He is not entirely sorry for the fresh need they have produced."

As the gospel of grace lays hold of us, something is radically right. We are living in truth and reality. We become as honest as the ninety-two-year-old priest who was venerated by everybody in town for his holiness. He was also a member of the Rotary Club. Every time the club met, he would be there, always on time and always seated in his favorite spot in a corner of the room.

One day the priest disappeared. It was as if he had vanished into thin air. The townsfolk searched all over and could find no trace of him. But the following month, when the Rotary Club met, he was there as usual sitting in his corner.

"Father," everyone cried, "where have you been?"

"I just served a thirty-day sentence in prison."

"In prison," they cried. "Father, you couldn't hurt a fly. What happened?"

"It's a long story," said the priest, "but briefly, this is what happened. I bought myself a train ticket to go into the city. I was standing on the platform waiting for the train to arrive when this stunningly beautiful girl appears on the arm of a policeman. She looked at me, turned to the cop and said, 'He did it. I'm certain he's the one who did it.' Well, to tell you the truth, I was so flattered I pleaded guilty."[5]

There's a touch of vanity in the holiest men and women. They see no reason to deny it. And they know that reality bites back if it isn't respected.

When I get honest, I admit I am a bundle of paradoxes. I believe and I doubt, I hope and I get discouraged, I love and I hate, I feel bad about feeling good, I feel guilty about not feeling guilty. I am trusting and suspicious. I am honest and I still play games. Aristotle said I am a rational animal; I say I am an angel with an incredible capacity for beer.

To live by grace means to acknowledge my whole life story, the light side and the dark. In admitting my shadow side I learn who I am and what God's grace means. As Thomas Merton put it, "A saint is not someone who is good but who experiences the goodness of God."

The gospel of grace nullifies our adulation of tele-vangelists, charismatic superstars, and local church heroes. It obliterates the two-class citizenship theory operative in many American churches. For grace proclaims the awesome truth that all is gift. All that is good is ours not by right but by the sheer bounty of a gracious God. While there is much we may have earned—our degree and our salary, our home and garden, a Miller Lite and a good night's sleep—all this is possible only because we have been given so much: life itself, eyes to see and hands to touch, a mind to shape ideas, and a heart to beat with love. We have been given God in our souls and Christ in our flesh. We have the power to believe where others deny, to hope where others despair, to love where others hurt. This and so much more is sheer gift; it is not reward for our faithfulness, our generous disposition, or our heroic life of prayer. Even our fidelity is a gift. "If we but turn to God," said St. Augustine, "that itself is a gift of God." My deepest awareness of myself is that I am deeply loved by Jesus Christ and I have done nothing to earn it or deserve it.

In my ministry as a vagabond evangelist, I have extolled certain saints and contemporary Christians, speaking of at what cost they have struggled to surpass lesser men and women. O God, what madness I have preached in sermons! The Good News of the Gospel of Grace cries out: we are all, equally, privileged but unentitled beggars at the door of God's mercy!

Besides, as Henri Nouwen notes, the greater part of God's work in the world may go unnoticed. There are a number of people who have become famous or widely known for their ministries, but much of God's saving activity in our history could remain completely unknown. That is a mystery difficult to grasp in an age that attaches so much importance to publicity. We tend to think that the more people know and talk about something, the more important it must be.

In Luke 18, a rich young man comes to Jesus asking what he must *do* to inherit eternal life. He wants to be in the spotlight. It is no coincidence that Luke juxtaposes the passage of Jesus and the children immediately preceding the verses on the young aristocrat. Children contrast with the rich man simply because there is no question of their having yet been able to merit anything. Jesus' point is: there is nothing that any of us can do to inherit the Kingdom. We must simply receive it like little children. And little children haven't done anything. The New Testament world was not sentimental about children and had no illusion about any pretended innate goodness in them. Jesus is not suggesting that heaven is a huge playground for Cajun infants. Children are our model because they have no claim on heaven. If they are close to God, it is because they are incompetent, not because they are innocent. If they receive anything, it can only be as a gift.

Paul writes in Ephesians: "It is by grace you have been saved through faith; not by anything of your own, but by a gift from God; not by anything you have done so that nobody can claim the credit" (2:8-9).

If a random sample of one thousand American Christians were taken today, the majority would define faith as belief in the existence of God. In earlier times it did not take faith to believe that God existed— almost everybody took that for granted. Rather, faith had to do with one's relationship to God—whether one trusted in God. The difference between faith as "belief in something that may or may not exist" and faith as "trusting in God" is enormous. The first is a matter of the head, the second a matter of the heart. The first can leave us unchanged, the second intrinsically brings change.[6]

Such is the faith described by Paul Tillich in his famous work *Shaking the Foundations*: "Grace strikes us when we are in great pain and restlessness. It strikes us when we walk through the dark valley of a meaningless and empty life. . . . It strikes us when, year after year, the longed-for perfection does not appear, when the old compulsions reign within us as they have for decades, when despair destroys all joy and courage. Sometimes at that moment a wave of light breaks into our darkness, and it is as though a voice were saying: 'You are accepted. You are accepted, accepted by that which is greater than you, and the name of which you do not know. Do not ask for the name now; perhaps you will find it later. Do not try to do anything now; perhaps later you will do much. Do not seek for anything, do not perform anything, do not intend anything. Simply accept the fact that you are accepted.' If that happens to us, we experience grace."[7]

And Grace calls out: you are not just a disillusioned old man who may die soon, a middle-aged woman stuck in a job and desperately wanting to get out, a young person feeling the fire in the belly begin to grow cold. You may be insecure, inadequate, mistaken, or potbellied. Death, panic, depression, and disillusionment may be near you. But you are not just that. You are accepted. Never confuse your perception of yourself with the mystery that you really are accepted.

Paul writes: "The Lord said, 'My grace is enough for you: my power is at its best in weakness.' So I shall be very happy to make my weaknesses my special boast so that the power of Christ may stay over me" (2 Corinthians 12:9). Whatever our failings may be, we need not lower our eyes in the presence of Jesus. Unlike Quasimodo, the hunchback of Notre Dame, we need not hide all that is ugly and repulsive in us. Jesus comes not for the super-spiritual but for the wobbly and the weak-kneed who know they don't have it all together, and who are not too proud to accept the handout of amazin' grace. As we glance up, we are astonished to find the eyes of Jesus open with wonder, deep with understanding, and gentle with compassion.

Something is radically wrong when the local church rejects a person accepted by Jesus: when a harsh, judgmental and unforgiving sentence is passed on homosexuals; when a divorcée is denied communion; when the child of a prostitute is refused baptism; when an unlaicized priest is forbidden the sacraments. Jesus comes to the ungodly, even on Sunday morning. His coming ends ungodliness and makes us worthy. Otherwise, we are establishing at the heart of Christianity an utterly ungodly and unworthy preoccupation with works.

Jesus sat down at table with anyone who wanted to be present, including those who were banished from decent homes. In the sharing of a meal they received consideration instead of the expected condemnation. A merciful acquittal instead of a hasty verdict of guilty. Amazing grace instead of universal disgrace. Here is a very practical demonstration of the law of grace—a new chance in life.

Any church that will not accept that it consists of sinful men and women, and exists for them, implicitly rejects the gospel of grace. As Hans Küng says, "It deserves neither God's mercy nor men's trust. The church must constantly be aware that its faith is weak, its knowledge dim, its profession of faith halting, that there is not a single sin or failing which it has not in one way or another been guilty of. *And though it is true that the church must always dissociate itself from sin, it can never have any excuse for keeping any sinners at a distance.* If the church remains self-righteously aloof from failures, irreligious and immoral people, it cannot enter justified into God's kingdom. But if it is constantly aware of its guilt and sin, it can live in joyous awareness of forgiveness. The promise has been given to it that anyone who humbles himself will be exalted."[8]

The story goes that a public sinner was excommunicated and forbidden entry to the church.

He took his woes to God, "They won't let me in, Lord, because I am a sinner."

"What are you complaining about?" said God. "They won't let me in either."

Often hobbling through our church doors on Sunday morning comes grace on crutches—sinners still unable to throw away their false supports and stand upright in the freedom of the children of God. Yet, their mere presence in the church on Sunday morning is a flickering candle representing a desire to maintain contact with God. To douse the flame is to plunge them into a world of spiritual darkness.

There is a myth flourishing in the church today that has caused incalculable harm—once converted, fully converted. In other words, once I accept Jesus Christ as my Lord and Savior, an irreversible, sinless future beckons. Discipleship will be an untarnished success story; life will be an unbroken upward spiral toward holiness. Tell that to poor Peter who, after three times professing his love for Jesus on the beach and after receiving the fullness of the Spirit at Pentecost, was still jealous of Paul's apostolic success.

Often I have been asked, "Brennan, how is it possible that you became an alcoholic after you got saved?" It is possible because I got battered and bruised by loneliness and failure, because I got discouraged, uncertain, guilt-ridden, and took my eyes off Jesus. Because the Christ-encounter did not transfigure me into an angel. Because justification by grace through faith means I have been set in right relationship with God, not made the equivalent of a patient etherized on a table.

We want eversharp spirituality (push-pull, click-click—one saint that quick) and attempt to cultivate a particular virtue at a given point in time. Prudence in January, humility in February, fortitude in March, temperance in April. Score cards are provided for toting up gains and losses. The losses should diminish if you expect to meet charity in May. Sometimes May never comes. For many Christians, life is a long January.

According to an ancient Christian legend, a saint once knelt down and prayed, "Dear God, I have only one desire in life. Give me the grace of never offending you again."

When God heard this, he started laughing out loud. "That's what they all ask for. But if I granted everyone this grace, tell me, whom would I forgive?"

Because salvation is by grace through faith, I believe that among the countless number of people standing in front of the throne and in front of the Lamb, dressed in white robes and holding palms in their hands (Revelation 7:9), I shall see the prostitute from the Kit-Kat Ranch in Carson City, Nevada, who tearfully told me she could find no other employment to support her two-year-old son. I shall see the woman who had an abortion and is haunted by guilt and remorse but did the best she could faced with grueling alternatives; the businessman besieged with debt who sold his integrity in a series of desperate transactions; the insecure clergyman addicted to being liked, who never challenged his people from the pulpit and longed for unconditional love; the sexually-abused teen molested by his father and now selling his body on the street, who, as he falls asleep each night after his last 'trick', whispers the name of the unknown God he learned about in Sunday school; the death-bed convert who for decades had his cake and ate it, broke every law of God and man, wallowed in lust and raped the earth.

"But how?" we ask. Then the voice says, "They have washed their robes and made them white in the blood of the Lamb."

There they are. There *we* are—the multitude who so wanted to be faithful, who at times got defeated, soiled by life, and bested by trials, wearing the bloodied garments of life's tribulations, but through it all clung to the faith.

My friends, if this is not good news to you, you have never understood the gospel of grace.

Chapter 2

Magnificent Monotony

Sir James Jeans, the famous British astronomer, once said, "The universe appears to have been designed by a Pure Mathematician." Joseph Campbell wrote of "a perception of a cosmic order, mathematically definable. . . ."

As they contemplate the order of the earth, the solar system, and the stellar universe, scientists and scholars have concluded that the Master Planner left nothing to chance.

The slant of the earth, for example, tilted at an angle of 23 degrees, produces our seasons. Scientists tell us that if the earth had not been tilted exactly as it is, vapors from the oceans would move both north and south, piling up continents of ice.

If the moon were only 50,000 miles away from earth instead of 200,000, the tides might be so enormous that all continents would be submerged in water—even the mountains would be eroded.

If the crust of the earth had been only ten feet thicker, there would be no oxygen, and without it all animal life would die.

Had the oceans been a few feet deeper, carbon dioxide and oxygen would have been absorbed and no vegetable life would exist.

The earth's weight has been estimated at six sextillion tons (that's a six with 21 zeros). Yet it is perfectly balanced and turns easily on its axis. It revolves daily at the rate of more than 1,000 miles per hour or 25,000 miles each day. This adds up to nine million miles a year. Considering the tremendous weight of six sextillion tons rolling at this fantastic speed around an invisible axis, held in place by unseen bands of gravitation, the words of Job 26:7 take on unparalleled significance: "He poised the earth on nothingness."

The earth revolves in its own orbit around the sun, making the long elliptical circuit of six hundred million miles each year—which means we are traveling in orbit at 19 miles per second or 1,140 miles per hour.

Job further invites us to meditate on "the wonders of God" (37:14). Consider the sun. Every square yard of the sun's surface is emitting constantly an energy level of 130,000 horse power (that is, approximately 450 eight-cylinder automobile engines), in flames that are being produced by an energy source much more powerful than coal.

The nine major planets in our solar system range in distance from the sun from 36 million to about 3 trillion, 6,664 billion miles; yet each moves around the sun in exact precision, with orbits ranging from 88 days for Mercury to 248 years for Pluto.

Still, the sun is only one minor star in the 100 billion orbs which comprise our Milky Way galaxy. If you were to hold out a dime, a ten-cent piece, at arm's length, the coin would block out 15 million stars from your view, if your eyes could see with that power.

When we attempt to comprehend the almost countless stars and other heavenly bodies in the Milky Way galaxy alone, we resonate to Isaiah's paean of praise to the all-powerful Creator: "Lift up your eyes and look. Who made these stars if not he who drills them like an army, calling each one by name? So mighty is his power, so great his strength, that not one fails to answer" (40:26).

Small wonder that David cries out: "Yahweh, our Lord, how great your name throughout the earth. Above the heaven is your majesty chanted, by the mouths of children, babes in arms. I look up at the heavens made by your fingers, at the moon and the stars you set in place—ah, what is man that you should spare a thought for him, the son of man that you should care for him?" (Psalm 8).[1]

Creation discloses a power that baffles our minds and beggars our speech. We are enamored and enchanted by God's power. We stutter and stammer about God's holiness. We tremble before God's majesty . . . and yet we grow squeamish and skittish before God's love.

I am flabbergasted by the widespread refusal across this land to think big about a loving God. Like nervous thoroughbreds being guided to the starting gate at Churchill Downs, many Christians bray, bridle, and bolt at the revelation of God's all-embracing love in Jesus Christ.

In my ministry as a vagabond evangelist, I have encountered shocking resistance to the God whom the Bible defines as Love. The skeptics range from the oily, over-polite professionals who discreetly drop hints of the heresy of universalism, to the Bible thumper who sees only the dusty, robust war God of the Pentateuch, and who insists on restating the cold demands of rule-ridden perfectionism.

Our resistance to the furious love of God may be traced to the church, our parents and pastors, and life itself. They have hidden the face of a compassionate God, we protest, and favored a God of holiness, justice, and wrath.

Yet, if we were truly men and women of prayer, our faces set like flint and our hearts laid waste by passion, we would discard our excuses. We would be done with blaming others.

We must go out into a desert of some kind (your backyard will do) and come into a personal experience of the awesome love of God. Then, we will nod in knowing agreement with that gifted English mystic Julian of Norwich: "The greatest honor we can give Almighty God is to live gladly because of the knowledge of his love." We shall understand why, as Kittel's *Theological Dictionary of the New Testament* notes, that in the last years of his life on the island of Patmos, the apostle John wrote, and wrote with *magnificent monotony,* of the love of Jesus Christ. As if for the first time, we shall grasp what Paul meant: "Where sin abounded, grace has more abounded; and so, just as sin reigned wherever there was death, so grace will reign to bring eternal life thanks to the righteousness that comes through Jesus Christ our Lord" (Romans 5:20-21).

Just as John in the twilight of his life wrote only of the love of Jesus, so Paul wrote lavishly of the gospel of grace:

- The grace of God is the totality by which men and women are made righteous (Romans 3:24; Titus 3:7).
- By grace Paul was called (Galatians 1:15).
- God bestows his glorious grace on us in his Son (Ephesians 1:6).
- The grace of God appeared for the salvation of all (Titus 2:11).
- The grace of our Lord has overflowed with the faith and love which are in Christ Jesus (1 Timothy 1:14).
- Grace is a store to which we have access through Christ (Romans 5:2).
- It is a state or condition in which we stand (Romans 5:2).
- It is received in abundance (Romans 5:17).
- The grace of God has abounded more than sin (Romans 5:15, 20-21, 6:1).
- It is given us in Christ (1 Corinthians 1:4).
- Paul did not receive it in vain (2 Corinthians 6:1).
- The surpassing grace of God is within the Christian (2 Corinthians 9:14).

- It extends to more and more people (2 Corinthians 4:15).

- Grace stands in opposition to works, which lack the power to save; if works had the power, the reality of grace would be annulled (Romans 11:5ff; Ephesians 2:5, 7ff; 2 Timothy 1:9).

- Grace stands in opposition to the law. Both Jews and Gentiles are saved through the grace of the Lord Jesus (Acts 15:11).

- To hold to the law is to nullify grace (Galatians 2:21); and when the Galatians accept the law, they have fallen from grace (Galatians 5:4).

- The Christian is not under the law but under grace (Romans 6:14ff).

- Grace is opposed to what is owed (Romans 4:4).

- The gospel itself, which is the good news of grace, can be called grace (Acts 20:24) or the word of his grace (Acts 14:3; 20:32).

Yes, the gracious God enfleshed in Jesus Christ *loves us*.

Grace is the active expression of his love. The Christian lives by grace as Abba's child, utterly rejecting the God who catches people by surprise in a sign of weakness—the God incapable of smiling at our awkward mistakes, the God who does not accept a seat at our human festivities, the God who says "You will pay for that," the God incapable of understanding that children will always get dirty and be forgetful, the God always snooping around after sinners.

At the same time, the child of the Father rejects the pastel-colored patsy God who promises never to rain on our parade.

A pastor I know recalls a Sunday morning Bible study at his church when the text under consideration was Genesis 22. God commands Abraham to take his son Isaac and offer him in sacrifice on Mount Moriah.

After the group read the passage, the pastor offered some historical background on this period in salvation-history, including the prevalence of child sacrifice among the Canaanites. The group listened in awkward silence.

Then the pastor asked, "But what does this story mean to us?"

A middle-aged man spoke up. "I'll tell you the meaning this story has for me. I've decided that me and my family are looking for another church."

The pastor was astonished, "What? Why?"

"Because," the man said, "when I look at that God, the God of Abraham, I feel I'm near a real God, not the sort of dignified, businesslike, Rotary Club God we chatter about here on Sunday mornings. Abraham's God could blow a man to bits, give and then take a child, ask for everything from a person, and then want more. I want to know that God."

The child of God knows that the graced life calls him or her to live on a cold and windy mountain, not on the flattened plain of reasonable, middle-of-the-road religion.

For at the heart of the gospel of grace, the sky darkens, the wind howls, a young man walks up another Moriah in obedience to a God who demands everything and stops at nothing. Unlike Abraham, he carries a cross on his back rather than sticks for the fire . . . like Abraham, listening to a wild and restless God who will have his way with us, no matter what the cost.

This is the God of the gospel of grace. A God, who out of love for us, sent the only Son he ever had wrapped in our skin. He learned how to walk, stumbled and fell, cried for his milk, sweated blood in the night, was lashed with a whip and showered with spit, was fixed to a cross and died whispering forgiveness on us all.

The God of the legalistic Christian, on the other hand, is often unpredictable, erratic, and capable of all manner of prejudices. When we view God this way, we feel compelled to engage in some sort of magic to appease him. Sunday worship becomes a superstitious insurance policy against his whims. This God expects people to be perfect and to be in perpetual control of their feelings and thoughts. When broken people with this concept of God fail—as inevitably they must—they usually expect punishment. So, they persevere in religious practices as they struggle to maintain a hollow image of a perfect self. The struggle itself is exhausting. The legalists can never live up to the expectations they project on God.

A married woman in Atlanta with two small children told me recently she was certain that God was disappointed with her because she wasn't "doing anything" for him. She told me she felt called to a soup kitchen ministry but struggled with leaving her children in someone else's care. She was shocked when I told her the call was not from God but from her own ingrained legalism. Being a good mother wasn't enough for her. In her mind, neither was it good enough for God.

In similar fashion, a person who thinks of God as a loose cannon firing random broadsides to let us know who's in charge will become fearful, slavish, and probably unbending in his or her expectations of others. If your God is an impersonal, cosmic force, your religion will be noncommittal and vague. The image of God as an omnipotent thug who brooks no human intervention creates a rigid lifestyle ruled by puritanical laws and dominated by fear.

But trust in the God who loves consistently and faithfully nurtures confident, free disciples. A loving God fosters a loving people. "The fact that our view of God shapes our lives to a great extent may be one of the reasons Scripture ascribes such importance to seeking to know him."[2]

This truth is illustrated in the prophet Jonah's view of God. Jonah is so outraged when the Ninevites repent after his preaching that he wants to die. He did not want God to forgive Ninevah; he wanted judgment. His narrow nationalism made it impossible for him to grasp the all-embracing love of God.[3] But the message of this prophetic book transcends the limits of the prophet. It proclaims how good God is, how his compassion extends to every creature in his universe, even as the last word in the book says, "to the animals." *All* men and women are the people of his caring. All are called to accept the extravagant gift of his grace, for acceptance means simply to turn to God.

Jonah could not handle that. He lost his cool, grew livid when a castor-oil plant that was his sunscreen withered, yet he could let thousands of people perish in their unbelief without turning pale. Not a bad guy. After all, he was willing to give up the ghost for pagan sailors. Not bad; just myopic. God was his God, the God of the Hebrews, imprisoned in one country, one temple, one ark of the covenant.

The theology of this sacred book is a clarion call to Israelites of both covenants: Think big about God. God's mercy on repentant Nineveh, on Jonah in his self-pity, even on brute animals, prepares the way for the gospel of grace: God is love.

"Over the years I've seen Christians shaping God in their own image—in each case a dreadfully small God. Some Roman Catholics still believe only they will graze heaven's green pastures. . . . There is the God who has a special affection for capitalist America, regards the workaholic, and the God who loves only the poor and the underprivileged. There is a God who marches with victorious armies, and the God who loves only the meek who turns the other cheek. Some like the elder brother in Luke, sulk and pout when the Father rocks and rolls, serves surf-and-turf for a prodigal son who has spent his last cent on whores. Some, tragically, refuse to believe that God can or will forgive them: My sin is too great."[4]

This is not the God of grace who "desires all men and women to be saved" (1 Timothy 2:4). This is not the God embodied in Jesus that Matthew came to know—the God who calls sinners—and you and I know, that means everybody.

I am reminded of a marvelous scene in Flannery O'Connor's short story "Revelation," based on the last book of the Bible. The main character is Mrs. Turpin, a self-righteous woman, proud of her good disposition, good deeds, and sense of decency. She has low regard for blacks and white trash. She hates freaks and the mentally ill. At night she would lie in bed and wonder who she would be if she couldn't have been herself.

"If Jesus had said to her before he made her, 'There's only two places available for you. You can either be a nigger or white trash. Which one?' She would have wiggled and squirmed and finally said: 'All right—make me a nigger then—but that don't mean a trashy one.' And he would have made her a neat, clean respectable Negro woman, herself but black."

Well, one day Mrs. Turpin goes to the doctor's office and finds herself surrounded by the people she despises. Suddenly a young woman with acne strides across the room, hits Mrs. Turpin with a book, and tries to strangle her. When order is finally restored, Mrs. Turpin, like she was awaiting a revelation, asks, "What you got to say to me?" And the young girl shouts: "Go back to hell where you came from, you old wart hog."

Mrs. Turpin is shattered. Her world has collapsed. The God she had fashioned in her own image, so pleased with her piety, has vanished.

She goes home and stands in her back yard staring at the pigpen. And she receives a vision. From the ground a brilliant, swinging, fiery bridge is raised from earth to heaven and along that bridge "a vast horde of souls were rumbling toward heaven. There were whole companies of white trash, clean for the first time in their lives, and bands of black niggers in white robes, and battalions of freaks and lunatics shouting and clapping and leaping like frogs" and finally a whole tribe of people just like herself "marching behind the others with great dignity, accountable as they had always been for good order and common sense and respectable behavior. They alone were on key. Yet she could see by their shocked and altered faces that even their virtues were being burned away."

The story ends with Mrs. Turpin going back into her house hearing only "the voices of the souls climbing upward into the starry field and shouting 'hallelujah.' "[5]

Perhaps a touch of Mrs. Turpin hides in a lot of holy people. A friend of mine once told me years ago that the one thing that made her uneasy about heaven is that she won't get to choose her table companions at the Messianic banquet.

Our experience of God's unconditional love must be shaped by the Scriptures. God's written Word must take hold of us as his spoken Word took hold of Isaiah and Jeremiah, Ezekiel and Hosea; as the spoken Word of Christ mesmerized Matthew and Mary Magdalene, and captivated Simon Peter and the Samaritan woman.

The Word we study has to be the Word we pray. My personal experience of the relentless tenderness of God came not from exegetes, theologians, and spiritual writers, but from sitting still in the presence of the living Word and beseeching him to help me understand with my head and heart his written Word. Sheer scholarship alone cannot reveal to us the gospel of grace. We must never allow the authority of books, institutions, or leaders to replace the authority of *knowing* Jesus Christ personally and directly. When the religious views of others interpose between us and the primary experience of Jesus as the Christ, we become unconvicted and unpersuasive travel agents handing out brochures to places we have never visited.

In his famous Christmas sermon in 1522, Martin Luther cried out: "O that God should desire that my interpretation and that of all teachers should disappear, and each Christian should come straight to the Scripture alone and to the pure word of God! You see from this babbling of mine the immeasurable difference between the word of God and all human words, and how no man can adequately reach and explain a single word of God with all his words. It is an eternal word and must be understood and contemplated with a quiet mind. No one else can understand except a mind that contemplates in silence. For anyone who could achieve this without commentary or interpretation, my commentaries and those of everyone else could not only be of no use, but merely a hindrance. Go to the Bible itself, dear Christians, and let my expositions and those of all scholars be no more than a tool with which to build aright, so that we can understand, taste and abide in the simple and pure word of God; for God dwells alone in Zion."[6]

Philosopher Jacques Maritain once said that the culmination of knowledge is not conceptual but experiential: I feel God. Such is the promise of the Scriptures: Be still and know (experience) that I am God. My own journey bears witness to that. I mean simply that a living, loving God can and does make his presence felt, can and does speak to us in the silence of our hearts, can and does warm and caress us till we no longer doubt that he is near, that he is here. Such experience is pure grace to the poor, the children and the sinners, the privileged types in the gospel of grace. It cannot be forced from God. He gives it freely, but he does give it and has given it to such as Moses and Matthew, to Roslyn and me. In fact, there is no one to whom God denies it. Ignatius of Loyola said: "The direct experience of God is grace indeed, and basically there is no one to whom it is refused."

In essence, there is only one thing God asks of us—that we be men and women of prayer, people who live close to God, people for whom God is everything and for whom God is enough. That is the root of peace. We have that peace when the gracious God is all we seek. When we start seeking something besides him, we lose it. As Merton said in the last public address before his death, "That is his call to us—simply to be people who are content to live close to him and to renew the kind of life in which the closeness is felt and experienced."

There was a time in my life when I knew nothing of this gracious God and his gospel of grace. Prior to my encounter with Jesus, my personal life was riddled with guilt, shame, fear, self-hatred, and obviously, low self-esteem. You see, growing up Catholic in the late 1930s and 1940s and 1950s, my central preoccupation was *sin*. Sin was everywhere. It consumed us and dominated our consciousness.

There were two kinds of sin, mortal, which was the more serious kind, and venial. Committing a mortal sin means knowing that what you are about to do, think, want, or say is really bad . . . but doing, thinking, wanting, or saying it anyway. Most of the things we did wrong fell into the less offensive category of venial sin. Committing a venial sin meant doing something that is not really so bad, or doing something really bad that you don't *think* is really bad or that your heart really isn't into doing. If your little brother is being a pest and you tell him to drop dead, you've committed a venial sin. If you shoot him dead, you've committed a mortal sin.

While the difference between mortal and venial sin seems obvious, don't be fooled. There is more to this than meets the eye. What is really bad and what isn't? And who decides? Here is a routine situation that every Catholic of my generation had to deal with: You are at a baseball game at Yankee Stadium on a Friday night in June 1950. Catholics are forbidden to eat meat under penalty of mortal sin. But you want a hot dog.

Now, just considering eating meat on Friday is a venial sin; wanting to is another one. You have not moved in your seat and you have already sinned twice. What if you actually ate one? Aside from the risk of choking on forbidden food and getting punished right on the spot, have you committed a mortal sin or a venial sin? Well, if you think it's mortal, it may be mortal; and if you think it's venial, it still may be mortal. After much thought, you decide it's venial. You call the hot dog vendor, you take the money out of your pocket, and you buy a hot dog. This is clearly an act of free will. You figure you can go confess your sin to the priest on Saturday night. But wait! Does a venial sin become mortal when you commit it deliberately? That's a chance you take. What if you've forgotten it's Friday? In that case, eating the hot dog may not be a sin, but forgetting it's Friday is. What if you remember it's Friday halfway through the hot dog? Is it a venial sin to finish it? If you throw it away, is wasting food a sin? Within five minutes you have committed enough sins to land you in purgatory for a million years. The simplest thing to do is not to take any chances—stay away from Yankee Stadium on Fridays.

Being a Catholic in those days meant a lifelong struggle to avoid sin, mortal or venial. While you didn't want to go to hell, you didn't want to rot in purgatory either. So play it safe. Think about every thought, word, action, desire, and omission. Figure that everything you want to do is a sin.[7]

In retrospect, while much of this stuff is hilarious, the sense of guilt and shame were terribly real. On a warm summer night in June 1947, I reached puberty. In the shower, I began to explore my body. For the first time, it tingled in response. I masturbated, panicked, threw on my clothes without drying off, raced to the local church, and confessed my sin. The priest thundered: "You did what? Do you know you could go to hell for that?" His voice boomed through the crowded church. I went home humiliated and frightened. (Since then, I have met many gentle, wise, and compassionate confessors, and the warm winds of spring are blowing through the Catholic Church after a long, cold winter).

Over the years, the growing consciousness of radical grace has wrought profound changes in my self-awareness. Justification by grace through faith means that I know myself accepted by God *as I am.* When my head is enlightened and my heart is pierced by this truth, I can accept myself as I am. Genuine self-acceptance is not derived from the power of positive thinking, mind-games,or pop psychology. *It is an act of faith* in the God of grace.

Several times in my ministry people have expressed the fear that self-acceptance will abort the ongoing conversion process and lead to a life of spiritual laziness and moral laxity. Nothing could be more untrue. The acceptance of self does not mean to be resigned to the status quo. On the contrary, the more fully we accept ourselves, the more successfully we begin to grow. Love is a far better stimulus than threat or pressure.

"One saint used to say that she was the type of woman who advances more rapidly when she is drawn by love than when driven by fear. She was perceptive enough to know that we are all that type of person. It is possible to attain great holiness of life while still being prone to pettiness and insincerity, sensuality and envy, but the first move will always be to recognize that I am that way. In terms of spiritual growth the faith-conviction that God accepts me as I am is a tremendous help to become better."[8]

When we accept ourselves for what we are, we decrease our hunger for power or the acceptance of others because our self-intimacy reinforces our inner sense of security. We are no longer preoccupied with being powerful or popular. We no longer fear criticism because we accept the reality of our human limitations. Once integrated, we are less often plagued with the desire to please others because simply being true to ourselves brings lasting peace. We are grateful for life and we deeply appreciate and love ourselves.

This chapter began with a paean of praise of the power of God manifested in the works of creation. The gospel of grace ends any apparent dichotomy between God's power and his love. For the work of creating is an act of love. The God who flung from his fingertips this universe filled with galaxies and stars, penguins and puffins, gulls and gannets, Pomeranians and poodles, elephants and evergreens, parrots and

potato bugs, peaches and pears, and a world full of
children made in his own image, is the God who loves
with magnificent monotony.

And anyone who has experienced the love of the
Lord of the Dance will tell you: the synonym for
monotonous is not *boring*.

Chapter 3

The Ragamuffin Gospel

After reading the entire Gospel of Luke for the first time, a post-Valley girl said: "Wow! Like Jesus has this totally intense thing for ragamuffins."

The young lady is onto something.

Jesus spent a disproportionate amount of time with people described in the gospels as: the poor, the blind, the lame, the lepers, the hungry, sinners, prostitutes, tax collectors, the persecuted, the downtrodden, the captives, those possessed by unclean spirits, all who labor and are heavy burdened, the rabble who know nothing of the law, the crowds, the little ones, the least, the last, and the lost sheep of the house of Israel.

In short, Jesus hung out with ragamuffins.

Obviously his love for failures and nobodies was not an exclusive love—that would merely substitute one class prejudice for another. He related with warmth and compassion to the middle and upper classes not because of their family connections, financial clout, intelligence, or Social Register status but because they, too, were God's children. While the term *poor* in the gospel includes the economically deprived and embraces all the oppressed who are dependent upon the mercy of others, it extends to all who rely entirely upon the mercy of God and accept the gospel of grace—the poor in spirit (Matthew 5:3).

Jesus' preference for little people and partiality toward ragamuffins is an irrefutable fact of the gospel narrative. As the French philosopher Maurice Blondel said: "If you really want to understand a man, don't just listen to what he says but watch what he does."

One of the mysteries of the gospel tradition is this strange attraction of Jesus for the unattractive, this strange desire for the undesirable, this strange love for the unlovely. The key to this mystery is, of course, Abba. Jesus does what he sees the Father doing, he loves those whom the Father loves.[1]

In his reply to the disciples' question about who is the greatest in the Kingdom of heaven (Matthew 18:1), Jesus abolished any distinction between the elite and the ordinary in the Christian community. "He called a little child to him and set the child in front of them. Then he said, 'I tell you solemnly, unless you change and become like little children, you will never enter the kingdom of heaven. And so, the one who makes himself as little as this little child is the greatest in the kingdom of heaven' " (Matthew 18:2-4).

Jesus cuts to the heart of the matter as he sits the child on his knee. The child is unself-conscious, incapable of pretense. I am reminded of the night little John Dyer, three years old, knocked on our door flanked by his parents. I looked down and said, "Hi, John. I am delighted to see you." He looked neither to the right nor left. His face was set like flint. He narrowed his eyes with the apocalyptic glint of an aimed gun. "Where's the cookies?" he demanded.

The Kingdom belongs to people who aren't trying to look good or impress anybody, even themselves. They are not plotting how they can call attention to themselves, worrying about how their actions will be interpreted or wondering if they will get gold stars for their behavior. Twenty centuries later, Jesus speaks pointedly to the preening ascetic trapped in the fatal narcissism of spiritual perfectionism, to those of us caught up in boasting about our victories in the vineyard, to those of us fretting and flapping about our human weaknesses and character defects. The child doesn't have to struggle to get himself in a good position for having a relationship with God; he doesn't have to craft ingenious ways of explaining his position to Jesus; he doesn't have to create a pretty face for himself; he doesn't have to achieve any state of spiritual feeling or intellectual understanding. All he has to do is happily accept the cookies: the gift of the Kingdom.

When Jesus tells us to become like little children, he is inviting us to forget what lies behind. Little John Dyer has no past. Whatever we have done in the past, be it good or evil, great or small, is irrelevant to our stance before God today. It is only *now* that we are in the presence of God.

The meaning of living in fidelity to the present moment, neither retreating to the past nor anticipating the future, is wonderfully illustrated by a Zen story about a monk being pursued by a ferocious tiger. He raced to the edge of the cliff, glanced back, and saw the growling tiger about to spring. The monk spotted a rope dangling over the edge of the cliff. He grabbed it and began shinning down the side of the cliff out of the clutches of the tiger. Whew! Narrow escape. He stared down and saw a huge quarry of jagged rocks five hundred feet below. He looked up and saw the tiger poised atop the cliff with bared claws. Just then, two mice began to nibble at the rope. What to do?

The monk saw a strawberry within arm's reach growing out of the face of the cliff side. He plucked it, ate it, and exclaimed, "Yum-yum; that's the best strawberry I've ever tasted in my entire life." If he had been preoccupied with the rock below (the future) or the tiger above (the past), he would have missed the strawberry God was giving him in the present moment. Children do not focus on the tigers of the past or the future but only on the strawberry that comes in *the here and now*.

The apostle Paul grasped the full meaning of Jesus' teaching on becoming like a little child. Serving as a coat rack during the stoning of Stephen and as a ringleader in the slaughter of Christians, Paul might well have become pathological had he dwelt on his pre-Christian past. But he writes, "All I can say is that I forget the past and I strain ahead for what is still to come" (Philippians 3:13).

Whatever past achievements might bring us honor, whatever past disgraces might make us blush, all have been crucified with Christ and exist no more except in the deep recesses of eternity, where "good is enhanced into glory and evil miraculously established as part of the greater good."[2]

It is important to remember the Jewish attitude toward children in first-century Palestine if we are to grasp the full force of Jesus' teaching here. In the present day, we tend to idealize childhood as the happy age of innocence, insouciance, and simple faith, but in New Testament times the child was considered of no importance, meriting little attention or favor. "Children in that society had no status at all—they did not count."[3] The child was regarded with scorn.

For the disciple of Jesus "becoming like a little child" means the willingness to accept oneself as being of little account and to be regarded as unimportant. The little child who is the image of the kingdom is a symbol of those who have the lowest places in society, the poor and the oppressed, the beggars, the prostitutes and tax collectors—the people whom Jesus often called the little ones or the least. Jesus' concern was that these little ones should not be despised or treated as inferior. "See that you never despise any of these little ones" (Matthew 18:10). He was well aware of their feelings of shame and inferiority, and because of his compassion they were, in his eyes, of extraordinarily great value. As far as he was concerned, they had nothing to fear. The kingdom was theirs. "There is no need to be afraid, little flock, for it has pleased your Father to give you the kingdom" (Luke 12:32).

Jesus gave these scorned little ones a privileged place in the kingdom and presented them as models to would-be disciples. They were to accept the kingdom in the same way the child would accept her allowance. If the children were privileged, it was not because they had merited privilege, but simply because God took pleasure in these little ones whom adults despised. The mercy of Jesus flowed out to them wholly from unmerited grace and divine preference.

The hymn of jubilation in Luke carries the same theme: "I bless you, Father, Lord of heaven and earth, for hiding these things from the wise and clever and revealing them to mere children. Yes, Father, for that is what it pleased you to do."

The scribes were treated with excessive deference in Jewish society because of their education and learning. Everyone honored them because of their wisdom and intelligence. The 'mere children' (*napioi* in Greek, really meaning babes) were Jesus' image for the uneducated and ignorant.[4] He is saying that the gospel of grace has been disclosed to and grasped by the uneducated and ignorant instead of the learned and wise. For this Jesus thanks God.

The babes (*napioi*) are in the same state as the children (*paidia*). God's grace falls on them because they are negligible creatures, not because of their good qualities. They may be aware of their worthlessness, but this is not the reason revelations are given to them. Jesus expressly attributes their good fortune to the Father's good pleasure, the divine *eudokia*. The gifts are not determined by the slightest personal quality or virtue. They were pure liberality. Once and for all, Jesus deals the death blow to any distinction between the elite and the ordinary in the Christian community.

Further light is cast on the ragamuffin gospel by the sinner's privilege. As I mentioned earlier, Jesus is seated at table in Levi's house. The scribes and pharisees badger him as to why he consorts with ragamuffins. Jesus said to them: "I have come to call sinners, not the self-righteous."

The sinners to whom Jesus directed his messianic ministry were not those who skipped morning devotions or Sunday church. His ministry was to those whom society considered *real* sinners. They had done nothing to merit salvation. Yet they opened themselves to the gift that was offered them. On the other hand, the self-righteous placed their trust in the works of the Law and closed their hearts to the message of grace.

But the salvation Jesus brought could not be earned. There could be no bargaining with God in a petty poker table atmosphere: "I have done this, therefore you owe me that." Jesus utterly destroys the juridic notion that our works demand payment in return. Our puny works do not entitle us to barter with God. Everything depends upon his good pleasure.

Several years ago I remember an angry letter written to the editor of a national evangelical magazine by an irate Catholic priest actively involved in the ministry of evangelism. He vehemently protested the cover story and picture of Francis MacNutt, also a Catholic priest with a worldwide healing ministry. MacNutt had recently married. The letter writer demanded to know why a previous article done on himself had been buried in the back of the magazine without a photo. He had stayed celibate all these years and had been given second-class treatment, while MacNutt, who had disobeyed the Pope and resigned the priesthood, was given star status. The author of the letter deemed the whole thing grossly unfair.

My wife, Roslyn, read his letter and remarked, "Shades of the elder brother of the prodigal son!"

However, this decided uneasiness with the ragamuffin gospel is not confined to one Christian tradition. In every denomination and non-denominational persuasion Christians are seeking to win God's favor by plunging into more spiritual activities, multiplying altars and sacrifices, making charitable contributions, lengthening the time of formal prayer, and getting involved in more church-related organizations.

There is need for careful discernment here. The evidence of earnestness, sincerity, and effort is considerable. The Christian's lifestyle is pious, proper, and correct. What's missing?

He or she has not surrendered to the Christ of grace.

The danger with our good works, spiritual investments, and all the rest of it is that we can construct a picture of ourselves in which we situate our self-worth. Complacency in ourselves then replaces sheer delight in God's unconditional love. Our doing becomes the very undoing of the ragamuffin gospel.

Nowhere in the New Testament is the privileged position of turkeys, nobodies, and marginal people on the fringes of society disclosed more dramatically than in Jesus' ministry of meal sharing.

In modern times it is scarcely possible to appreciate the scandal Jesus caused by his table fellowship with sinners. "In the year 1925, if a wealthy plantation owner in Atlanta extended a formal invitation to four colored cotton pickers to come to his mansion for Sunday dinner, preceded by cocktails and followed by several hours of brandy and conversation, the Georgia aristocracy would have been outraged, neighboring Alabama infuriated, and the Ku Klux Klan apoplectic. Sixty or seventy years ago in the deep South, the caste system was inviolable, social and racial discrimination inflexible, and indiscretion made the loss of reputation inevitable."[5]

In first century Palestinian Judaism the class system was enforced rigorously. It was legally forbidden to mingle with sinners who were outside the law: table fellowship with beggars, tax collectors (traitors to the national cause because they were collecting taxes *for* Rome from their own people to get a kick-back from the take) and prostitutes was a religious, social, and cultural taboo.

Sadly, the meaning of meal sharing is largely lost in the Christian community today. In the Near East, to share a meal with someone is a guarantee of peace, trust, fraternity, and forgiveness: the shared table symbolizes a shared life. For an orthodox Jew to say, "I would like to have dinner with you," is a metaphor implying "I would like to enter into friendship with you." Even today an American Jew will share a donut and a cup of coffee with you, but to extend a dinner invitation is to say: "Come to my *mikdash me-at,* the miniature sanctuary of my dining room table where we will celebrate the most sacred and beautiful experience that life affords—friendship." That is what Zacchaeus heard when Jesus called him down from the sycamore tree, and that is why Jesus' practice of table fellowship caused hostile comment from the outset of his ministry.

It did not escape the Pharisees's attention that Jesus meant to befriend the rabble. He was not only breaking the law, he was destroying the very structure of Jewish society. "They all complained when they saw what was happening. He has gone to stay at a sinner's house, they said" (Luke 19:7). But Zacchaeus, not too hung up on respectability, was overwhelmed with joy.

"It would be impossible to overestimate the impact these meals must have had upon the poor and the sinners. By accepting them as friends and equals Jesus had taken away their shame, humiliation, and guilt. By showing them that they mattered to him as people he gave them a sense of dignity and released them from their old captivity. The physical contact which he must have had with them at table (John 13:25) and which he obviously never dreamed of disallowing (Luke 7:38-39) must have made them feel clean and acceptable. Moreover because Jesus was looked upon as a man of God and a prophet, they would have interpreted his gesture of friendship as God's approval on them. They were now acceptable to God. Their sinfulness, ignorance, and uncleanness had been overlooked and were no longer being held against them."[6]

Through table fellowship Jesus ritually acted out his insight into Abba's indiscriminate love—a love that causes his sun to rise on bad men as well as good, and his rain to fall on honest and dishonest men alike (Matthew 5:45). The inclusion of sinners in the community of salvation, symbolized in table fellowship, is the most dramatic expression of the ragamuffin gospel and the merciful love of the redeeming God.

Thorough biblical research indicates that Jesus either had his own home in Capernaum or at least shared one with Peter, Andrew, and their families.

Undoubtedly, in his ministry as an itinerant evangelist, Jesus often slept on the side of the road or stayed with friends. "The Son of man has nowhere to lay his head" (Matthew 8:20). But we may have taken this statement too literally. "It is difficult to understand how Jesus could have been accused of entertaining sinners (Luke 15:2) if he did not have some kind of home in which to do so."[7]

Upon returning home from his missionary journeys, Jesus probably had some kind of quasi-permanent residence wherein he often served as host. Meal sharing occurred with such regularity that Jesus was accused of being a drunkard and a glutton (Luke 7:34). The guest list would include a ragtag parade of donkey peddlers, prostitutes, herdsmen, slumlords, and gamblers. A social climber Jesus was not.

Status seekers today are selective about their dinner guests and make elaborate preparations (linen, china, silver, fresh flowers, an exquisite Beaujolais, truffle sauce, Long Island duck under glazed raspberry, death-by-chocolate dessert, and so on) for people they want to stand well with. Then they anxiously await the morning mail to see if their dinner invitation is reciprocated.

Consciously or unconsciously, the social gadflies of our day do not underestimate the ritual power of meal sharing. Jesus' sinner guests were well aware that table fellowship entailed more than mere politeness or courtesy. It meant peace, acceptance, reconciliation, and brotherhood. "For Jesus this fellowship at table with those whom the devout had written off was not merely the expression of liberal tolerance and humanitarian sentiment. It was the expression of his mission and message: peace and reconciliation for all, without exception, even for the moral failures."[8]

The gospel portrait of Jesus is that of a person who cherished life and especially other people as loving gifts from the Father's hand. The peripheral figures whom Jesus encountered in his ministry reacted in various ways to his person and his message, but few responded with gloom or sadness. (And they were those such as the rich young ruler who rejected his message.) The living presence of Jesus awakened joy and set people free. Joy was in fact the most characteristic result of all his ministry to ragamuffins.

"One day when John's disciples and the Pharisees were fasting, some people came and said to him, 'Why is it that John's disciples and the disciples of the Pharisees fast, but your disciples do not?' Jesus replied, 'Surely the bridegroom's attendants would never think of fasting while the bridegroom is still with them? As long as they have the bridegroom with them, they could not think of fasting' " (Mark 2:18-19).

Jesus feasted while John fasted. Whereas John's call to conversion was essentially linked to penitential practices, the call of Jesus is fundamentally connected to being a table companion, eating and drinking with Jesus in whom God's merciful manner with sinners is manifested. Breaking bread with Jesus was a festive celebration of good fellowship in which there was salvation. Asceticism was not only inappropriate but unthinkable in the presence of the Bridegroom.

This remarkable passage illuminates the extraordinary enchantment cast by the Carpenter-Messiah. The ragamuffins discovered that sharing a meal with him was a liberating experience of sheer joy. He freed them from self-hatred, exhorted them not to confuse their perception of themselves with the mystery they really were, gave them what they needed more than anything else—encouragement for their lives—and delivered reassuring words such as "Do not live in fear, little flock; don't be afraid; fear is useless, what is needed is trust; stop worrying; cheer up—your sins are all forgiven." Small wonder that the evangelist Mark preserved this memory of Jesus with the utmost care.

The contagious joy of Jesus (only carriers can pass it on) infected and freed his followers. The author of Hebrews says: "Jesus Christ is the same yesterday, today, and forever" (13:8). If Jesus appeared at your dining room table tonight with knowledge of everything you are and are not, total comprehension of your life story and every skeleton hidden in your closet; if he laid out the real state of your present discipleship with the hidden agenda, the mixed motives, and the dark desires buried in your psyche, you would feel his acceptance and forgiveness. For "experiencing God's love in Jesus Christ means experiencing that one has been unreservedly accepted, approved and infinitely loved, that one can and should accept oneself and one's neighbor. Salvation is joy in God which expresses itself in joy in and with one's neighbor."[9]

Therefore, it is unimaginable to picture a wooden faced, stoic, joyless, and judgmental Jesus as he reclined with ragamuffins. The human personality of Jesus is underrated when it is perceived as a passive mask for the dramatic speeches of divinity. Such timidity robs Jesus of his humanity, encases him in plaster of paris, and concludes that he neither laughed, cried, smiled, nor got hurt but simply passed through our world without emotional engagement.

Mark records that a group of parents, who obviously sensed something of God's love in Jesus, wanted him to bless their little ones. The irritated disciples, fatigued by the long day's journey on foot from Capernaum to the district of Judea and the far side of the Jordan, attempted to shoo away the children. Jesus became visibly upset and silenced the Twelve with a withering glance. Mark notes carefully that Jesus picked them up *one by one*, cradled them, and gave each of them his blessing.

My friend Robert Frost comments: "I am so glad Jesus didn't suggest they group all the children together for a sort of general blessing because he was tired. Instead he took time to hold each child close to his heart and to earnestly pray for them all . . . then they joyfully scampered off to bed. One is tenderly reminded of a beautiful messianic passage from the prophets. 'He will feed his flock like a shepherd, he will gather the lambs in his arms, he will carry them in his bosom, and will gently lead those that have their young' (Isaiah 40:11). I think there is a lesson here for anyone who would seek to set any kind of false condition concerning *just who should be the recipients of God's grace. He blessed them all.*"[10]

A brief digression: there is a wondrous open-mindedness about children and an insatiable desire to learn from life. An open attitude is like an open door—a welcoming disposition toward the fellow travelers who knock on our door during the middle of a day, the middle of the week, or the middle of a lifetime. Some are dirtballs, grungy, disheveled, and bedraggled. The sophisticated adult within me shudders and is reluctant to offer them hospitality. They may be carrying precious gifts under their shabby rags, but I still prefer clean-shaven Christians who are neatly attired, properly pedigreed, and who affirm my vision, echo my thoughts, stroke me, and make me feel good. Yet, my inner child protests: "I want new friends, not old mirrors."

When our inner child is not nurtured and nourished, our minds gradually close to new ideas, unprofitable commitments, and the surprises of the Spirit. Evangelical faith is bartered for cozy, comfortable piety. A failure of nerve and an unwillingness to risk distorts God into a Bookkeeper and the gospel of grace is swapped for the security of religious bondage.

"Unless you become as little children . . . " Heaven will be filled with five-year-olds.

Burkhardt writes: "I fear for the lawyer whose only life is corporate tax, the doctor whose whole existence is someone else's prostate, the business executive whose single responsibility is to his stockholders, the athlete who puts all his eggs in an 18-inch basket, the theologian who thinks the world can be saved by theology. . . . A closed mind kills marriages and human relations; it deadens feelings and sensitivities; it makes for a church that lives in a thousand and one tunnels, with no communication and no exit."[11]

If we maintain the open-mindedness of children, we challenge fixed ideas and established structures, including our own. We listen to people in other denominations and religions. We don't find demons in those with whom we disagree. We don't cozy up to people who mouth our jargon. If we are open, we rarely resort to either-or: either creation or evolution, liberty or law, sacred or secular, Beethoven or Madonna. We focus on both-and, fully aware that

God's truth cannot be imprisoned in a small definition. Of course, the open mind does not accept everything indiscriminately—Marxism and capitalism, Christianity and atheism, love and lust, Moët Chandon and vinegar. It does not absorb all propositions equally like a sponge; nor is it as soft. But the open mind realizes that reality, truth, and Jesus Christ are incredibly open-ended. (Digression foreclosed).

The ragamuffin spirit of Jesus sometimes surfaces in the most unlikely settings and is often totally absent in places we most expect to find it. Let me close this chapter with a tale of two communities—both cut close to the bone of my existence: one concerns alcoholics, the other involves Roslyn.

On a sweltering summer night in New Orleans, sixteen recovering alcoholics and drug addicts gather for their weekly AA meeting. Although several members attend other meetings during the week, this is their home group. They have been meeting on Tuesday nights for several years and know each other well. Some talk to each other daily on the telephone, others socialize outside the meetings. The personal investment in one another's sobriety is sizable. Nobody fools anybody else. Everyone is there because he or she made a slobbering mess of his or her life and is trying to put the pieces back together. Each meeting is marked by levity and seriousness. Some members are wealthy, others middle class or poor. Some smoke, others don't. Most drink coffee. Some have graduate degrees, others have not finished high school. For one small hour the high and the mighty descend and the lowly rise. The result is fellowship.

The meeting opened with the Serenity Prayer followed by a moment of silence. The prologue to

Alcoholics Anonymous was read from the Big Book by Harry followed by the Twelve Steps of the program from Michelle. That night, Jack was the appointed leader. "The theme I would like to talk about tonight is gratitude," he began, "but if anyone wants to talk about something else, let's hear it."

Immediately Phil's hand shot up. ,

"As you all know, last week I went up to Pennsylvania to visit family and missed the meeting. You also know I have been sober for seven years. Last Monday I got drunk and stayed drunk for five days."

The only sound in the room was the drip of Mr. Coffee in the corner.

"You all know the buzz word, H.A.L.T., in this program," he continued. "Don't let yourself get hungry, angry, lonely, or tired or you will be very vulnerable for the first drink. The last three got to me. I unplugged the jug and . . ."

Phil's voice choked and he lowered his head. I glanced around the table—moist eyes, tears of compassion, soft sobbing the only sound in the room.

"The same thing happened to me, Phil, but I stayed drunk for a year."

"Thank God you're back."

"Boy, that took a lot of guts."

"Relapse spells relief, Phil," said a substance abuse counselor. "Let's get together tomorrow and figure out what you needed relief from and why."

"I'm so proud of you."

"Hell, I never made even close to seven years."

As the meeting ended, Phil stood up. He felt a hand on his shoulder, another on his face. Then kisses on his eyes, forehead, neck, and cheek. "You old ragamuffin," said Denise. "Let's go. I'm treating you to a banana split at Tastee-Freeze."

The second scenario occurred when Roslyn was taking a graduate course in religious education at Loyola University in New Orleans in the summer of 1981.

Dr. Meghan McKenna was lecturing on the New Testament milieu in which Jesus' ministry began. The four dominant religious groups were the Pharisees, Sadducees, Zealots, and Essenes. The Pharisees separated themselves from everyone who was not faithful to the law and the traditions, in order to form closed communities, the faithful remnant of Israel. Their name means 'the separate ones', i.e., the holy ones, the true community of Israel. Their morality was legalistic and bourgeois, a matter of reward and punishment. God loved and rewarded those who kept the law and hated and punished those who did not.

Dr. McKenna discussed the position of the Sadducees, mostly conservative and largely composed of the wealthy aristocracy; the Zealots who viewed submission to Rome as an act of unfaithfulness to God; the Essenes who rejected everyone who did not belong to their sect. They separated themselves completely from society and lived a celibate and ascetic life in the desert. All outsiders were to be hated as the sons of darkness. Love and respect were reserved for members of their group—the sons of light.

The "sinners," McKenna continued, were social outcasts. Anyone who for any reason deviated from the law and the customs of the middle class (the educated and virtuous, the Scribes and Pharisees) was treated as inferior, as low class. The sinners were a well-defined social group.

As her lecture ended, Dr. McKenna suggested: "Let's do a little exercise right here in the classroom. Would all those who do not smoke stand up, walk to the left and stand by the wall. And reformed smokers stand in the center of the room. Those who still smoke form a group on the right."

Thirty of the professionals had never smoked, twelve were reformed, three were active smokers. "At that time," Roslyn said, "I belonged to the latter group. An immediate sense of separation was obvious."

"Let's discuss two questions," McKenna said. "First, how do you feel about the current smoking regulations on campus, in restaurants, airports, the corporate world, and so forth?"

All three groups unanimously agreed that the regulations were good, ecologically important, and sensitive to the health and welfare of others.

"The second question: How do you feel about smokers personally?"

"They are disgusting and inconsiderate," said one nonsmoker.

"Obviously anyone who smokes has low self-esteem and a lousy self-image," voiced another.

"They have no will power."

"Rotten role models for teenagers."

"I have serious questions about the quality of their faith and depth of their personal relationship with Christ."

"Don't they know they are poisoning the atmosphere?"

Roslyn: "I cowered against the far wall feeling like the woman caught in adultery. Suddenly the environment was so hostile. For the past four years of graduate school, I had prayed, worshiped, gone on picnics, taken coffee breaks, studied, and conversed with these people. I felt a deep sense of bonding because of our shared life and ministry. The reformed smokers were much more understanding because they had been there—the place of addiction. At first, I was angry. When the inner rage finally subsided, I wanted to weep. I have never felt so alone.

"The bell sounded and class ended. We filed out of the room in silence."

The next day Dr. McKenna, following her usual procedure, asked her students to share their feelings and reactions to the exercise of the previous day.

"Yesterday I learned something about myself," said the woman who had made the harshest and most judgmental comments during the exercise. "I need a lot more compassion for people who are different from myself."

"How did you feel yesterday, Roslyn?" inquired the teacher.

"When I was standing against the wall, I actually thought the Group #1 people would have thrown stones at us were they available. I realized how difficult it was for me to look at them and say, 'Father, forgive them for they know not what they do.' "

Dr. McKenna's exercise achieved what it set out to accomplish. The fierce words of Jesus addressed to the Pharisees of his day stretch across the bands of time. Today they are directed not only to fallen televangelists but to each of us. We miss Jesus' point entirely when we use his words as weapons against others. They are to be taken personally by each of us.

This is the form and shape of Christian Pharisaism in our time. Hypocrisy is not the prerogative of people in high places. The most impoverished among us is capable of it. "Hypocrisy is the natural expression of what is meanest in us all."[12]

The ragamuffin gospel reveals that Jesus forgives sins—including sins of the flesh—that he is comfortable with sinners who remember how to show compassion, but that he cannot and will not have a relationship with pretenders in the Spirit.

Perhaps the real dichotomy in the Christian community today is not between conservatives and liberals or creationists and evolutionists but between the awake and the asleep. The Christian ragamuffin acknowledges with MacBeth: "Life is but a poor player that struts and frets his hour upon the stage, and then is heard no more." Just as a smart man knows he is stupid, so the awake Christian knows he/she is a ragamuffin.

Although truth is not always humility, humility is always truth: the blunt acknowledgment that I owe my life, being, and salvation to Another. This fundamental act lies at the core of our response to grace.

The beauty of the ragamuffin gospel lies in the insight it offers into Jesus: the essential tenderness of his heart, his way of looking at the world, his mode of relating to you and me. "If you really want to understand a man, don't just listen to what he says, but watch what he does."

Chapter 4

Tilted Halos

A man walked into the doctor's office and said, "Doctor, I have this awful headache that never leaves me. Could you give me something for it?"

"I will," said the doctor, "but I want to check a few things out first. Tell me, do you drink a lot of liquor?"

"Liquor?" said the man indignantly. "I never touch the filthy stuff."

"How about smoking?"

"I think smoking is disgusting. I've never in my life touched tobacco."

"I'm a bit embarrassed to ask this, but—you know the way some men are—do you do any running around at night?"

"Of course not. What do you take me for? I'm in bed every night by ten o'clock at the latest."

"Tell me," said the doctor, "the pain in the head you speak of, is it a sharp, shooting kind of pain?"

"Yes," said the man. "That's it—a sharp, shooting kind of pain."

"Simple, my dear fellow! Your trouble is you have your halo on too tight. All we need to do is loosen it a bit."[1]

The trouble with our ideals is that if we live up to all of them, we become impossible to live with.

The tilted halo of the saved sinner is worn loosely and with easy grace. We have discovered that the cross accomplished far more than revealing the love of God. The blood of the Lamb points to the truth of grace: what we cannot do for ourselves, God has done for us. On the cross, somehow, some way, Christ bore our sins, took our place, died for us. At the cross, Jesus unmasks the sinner not only as a *beggar* but as a *criminal* before God. Jesus Christ bore our sins and bore them away. We cannot wash away the stain of our sins, but he is the Lamb who has taken away the sins of the world.

The sinner saved by grace is haunted by Calvary, by the cross, and especially by the question: Why did he die? A clue comes from the Gospel of John: "God loved the world so much that He gave his only Son, that whoever believes in him should not perish but have eternal life." Another clue from Paul's cry in Galatians: "He loved me and delivered himself up for me." The answer lies in love.

But the answer seems too easy, too glib. Yes,

God saved us because he loved us. But he is God. He has infinite imagination. Couldn't he have dreamed up a different redemption? Couldn't he have saved us with a smile, a pang of hunger, a word of forgiveness, a single drop of blood? And if he had to die, then for God's sake—for Christ's sake—couldn't he have died in bed, died with dignity? Why was he condemned like a criminal? Why was his back flayed with whips? Why was his head crowned with thorns? Why was he nailed to wood and allowed to die in frightful, lonely agony? Why was the last breath drawn in bloody disgrace, while the world for which he lay dying egged on his executioners with savage fury like some kind of gang rape by uncivilized brutes in Central Park? Why did they have to take the very best?

One thing we do know—we don't comprehend the love of Jesus Christ. Oh, we see a movie and resonate to what a young man and woman will endure for romantic love. We know that when the chips are down, if we love wildly enough we'll fling life and caution to the winds for the one we love. But when it comes to God's love in the broken, blood-drenched body of Jesus Christ, we get antsy and start to talk about theology, divine justice, God's wrath, and the heresy of universalism.

The saved sinner is prostrate in adoration, lost in wonder and praise. He knows repentance is not what we do in order to earn forgiveness; it is what we do because we have been forgiven. It serves as an expression of gratitude rather than an effort to earn forgiveness. Thus the sequence of forgiveness and then repentance, rather than repentance and then forgiveness, is crucial for understanding the gospel of grace.

But many of us don't know our God and don't understand his gospel of grace. For many, God sits up there like a Buddha, impassive, unmoving, hard as flint. Calvary cries out more clearly than any theology textbook: We do not know our God. We have not grasped the truth in the First Letter of John: "In this is love, not that we loved God but that He loved us and sent his Son to be the propitiation for our sins." The cross reveals the depth of the Father's love for us: "For greater love than this no one has than that he lay down his life for his friends."

The disciple living by grace rather than law has undergone a decisive conversion—*a turning from mistrust to trust.* The foremost characteristic of living by grace is trust in the redeeming work of Jesus Christ.

To believe deeply, as Jesus did, that God is present and at work in human life is to understand that I am a beloved child of this Father and hence, *free to trust.* That makes a profound difference in the way I relate to myself and others; it makes an enormous difference in the way I live. To trust Abba, both in prayer and life, is to stand in childlike openness before a mystery of gracious love and acceptance.[2]

The tendency in legalistic religion is to mistrust God, to mistrust others, and consequently to mistrust ourselves. Allow me to become personal for a moment. Do you really believe that the Father of our Lord and Savior Jesus Christ is gracious, that he cares about you? Do you really believe that he is always, unfailingly, present to you as companion and support? Do you really believe that God is love?

Or have you learned to fear this loving and gracious Father? "In love," John says, "there can be no fear, for fear is driven out by perfect love. Fear has to do with punishment and anyone who is afraid is still imperfect in love" (1 John 4:18). Have you learned to think of the Father as the judge, the spy, the disciplinarian, the punisher? If you think that way, you are wrong.

The Father's love is revealed in the Son's. The Son has been given to us that we might give up fear. There is no fear in love. The Father sent the Son "that you might have life—life in all its fullness" (John 10:10). Is not the Son the Father's unsurpassable sign of love and graciousness? Did he not come to show us the Father's compassionate care for us? ("Whoever sees me sees also him who sent me" [John 12:45].) The Father is not justice and the Son love. The Father is justice *and* love; the Son is love *and* justice.

Abba is not our enemy. If we think that, we are wrong.

Abba is not intent on trying and tempting and testing us. If we think that, we are wrong.

Abba does not prefer and promote suffering and pain. If we think that, we are wrong.

Jesus brings good news about the Father, not bad news.

We need a new kind of relationship with the Father that drives out fear and mistrust and anxiety and guilt, that permits us to be hopeful and joyous, trusting and compassionate. We have to be converted from the bad news to the good news, from expecting nothing to expecting something.[3] "The right time has come," Jesus said, "and the Kingdom of God is near. Turn away from your sins and believe the Good

News" (Mark 1:15). Turn away from the sins of skepticism and despair, mistrust and cynicism, complaining and worry.

The gospel of grace calls us to sing of the everyday mystery of intimacy with God instead of always seeking for miracles or visions. It calls us to sing of the spiritual roots of such commonplace experiences as falling in love, telling the truth, raising a child, teaching a class, forgiving each other after we have hurt each other, standing together in the bad weather of life, of surprise and sexuality, and the radiance of existence.[4] Of such is the kingdom of heaven, and of such homely mysteries is genuine religion made. The conversion from mistrust to trust is a confident quest seeking the spiritual meaning of human existence. Grace abounds and walks around the edges of our everyday experience.

Trust defines the meaning of living by grace rather than works. Trust is like climbing a fifty-foot ladder, reaching the top, and hearing someone down below yell "Jump." The trusting disciple has this childlike confidence in a loving Father. Trust says, in effect, "Abba, just on the basis of what you have shown me in your son, Jesus, I believe you love me. You have forgiven me. You will hold me and never let me go. Therefore, I trust you with my life."

Donald McCullough puts it this way: "Grace means that in the middle of our struggle the referee blows the whistle and announces the end of the game. We are declared winners and sent to the showers. It's over for all huffing, puffing piety to earn God's favor; it's finished for all sweat-soaked straining to secure self-worth; it's the end of all competitive scrambling to get ahead of others in the game. Grace means that God is on our side and thus we are victors regardless of how well we have played the game. We might as well head for the showers and the champagne celebration."[5]

The gospel declares that no matter how dutiful or prayerful we are, we can't save ourselves. What Jesus did was sufficient. To the extent that we are self-made saints like the Pharisees or neutral like Pilate (never making the leap in trust), we let the prostitutes and publicans go first into the kingdom while we, in Flannery O'Connor's unforgettable image, are in the background having our alleged virtue burnt out of us. The hookers and swindlers enter before us because they know they cannot save themselves, they cannot make themselves presentable or lovable. They risked everything on Jesus, and knowing they didn't have it all together, were not too proud to accept the handout of amazing grace.

Maybe this is the heart of our hang-up, the root of our dilemma. We fluctuate between castigating ourselves and congratulating ourselves because we are deluded into thinking we save ourselves. We develop a false sense of security from our good works and scrupulous observance of the law. Our halo gets too tight and a carefully-disguised attitude of moral superiority results. *Or*, we are appalled by our inconsistency, devastated that we haven't lived up to our lofty expectations of ourselves. The roller coaster ride of elation and depression continues.

Why?

Because we never lay hold of our nothingness before God, and consequently, we never enter into the deepest reality of our relationship with him. But when we accept ownership of our powerlessness and help-lessness, when we'acknowledge that we are paupers at the door of God's mercy, then God can make some-thing beautiful out of us.

This poverty of spirit is the second major charac-teristic of saved sinners with tilted halos living by grace. What is the person canonized by Jesus in the first beatitude ("Blessed are those who know that they are poor") really like?

A story: Several years ago, at the end of a parish renewal in Algiers, Louisiana, a man about forty approached me outside the church, muttered "I've prayed about this," slipped an envelope in my pocket, and hurried away. I was overdue at a reception in the parish hall, so I jogged over to converse with folks, completely forgetting the envelope. Late that night in preparing for bed, I emptied my pockets, opened the envelope, and a check for six thousand dollars fell to the floor.

Prior to that renewal, I had lived for a few days at the city garbage dump in Juarez, Mexico, where little children and old men and women literally scavenged food from a mound of refuse more than thirty feet high. Several children died each week because of mal-nutrition and polluted water. I sent the six-thousand-dollar check to a man with ten children, three of whom had already died from the grinding poverty and wretched living conditions. Do you know what the man who received the check did?

He wrote me nine letters in two days—letters overflowing with gratitude describing in detail how he was using the money to help his own family and other neighbors at the dump. That gave me a beautiful insight into what a poor man is like.

When he receives a gift, he first experiences, then expresses genuine gratitude. Having nothing, he appreciates the slightest gift. I have been given the utterly undeserved gift of salvation in Jesus Christ. Through no merit of mine, I have been given a bona fide invitation to drink new wine forever at the wedding feast in the Kingdom of God. (Incidentally, for a recovering alcoholic, that's heaven!)

But sometimes I get so involved with myself that I start making demands for things I think I deserve, or I take for granted every gift that comes my way. Classic case: man in restaurant orders crabmeat salad; mistakenly, waitress brings shrimp salad; livid, angry man roars: "Where the hell's my crabmeat?" Somehow, life owes him a crabmeat salad. He takes for granted not only the shrimp salad but so many other gifts—life, faith, family, friends, talents.

The deeper we grow in the Spirit of Jesus Christ, the poorer we become—the more we realize that everything in life is a gift. The tenor of our lives becomes one of humble and joyful thanksgiving. Awareness of our poverty and ineptitude causes us to rejoice in the gift of being called out of darkness into wondrous light and translated into the Kingdom of God's beloved Son. The poor man and woman write nine letters to the Lord that cry out, "It is right."

In conversation, the disciple who is truly poor in spirit always leaves the other person with the feeling, "My life has been enriched by talking with you." This is neither false modesty nor phony humility. His or her life has been enriched and graced. He is not all exhaust and no intake. She does not impose herself on others. He listens well because he knows he has so much to learn from others. Her spiritual poverty enables her to enter the world of the other even when she cannot identify with that world: i.e., the drug culture, the gay world. The poor in spirit are the most nonjudgmental of peoples; they get along well with sinners.

The poor man and woman of the gospel have made peace with their flawed existence. They are aware of their lack of wholeness, their brokenness, the simple fact that they don't have it all together. While they do not excuse their sin, they are humbly aware that sin is precisely what has caused them to throw themselves at the mercy of the Father. They do not pretend to be anything but what they are: sinners saved by grace.

The person who is poor in spirit realizes that he or she does not love others as much as his or her heart would wish. I once preached six week-long Lenten renewals in succession. The last was in Downers Grove, Illinois, and on the closing night I was wiped out. Over one thousand people had attended. As the recessional song signaling my exit from the church began, I debated internally whether my body could handle another half-hour of farewells and blessings in the vestibule.

An attractive alternative loomed. I could flee to the sacristy, divest myself of the ministerial robes, grab a cold drink, run to my room, and crash. Spirit willing but flesh rebelling. Finally, I prayed for a zap of the Holy Spirit, opted for the farewells in the parish hall, got into it as best I could, and hit the boards around midnight.

The next morning, a note addressed to me lay on the breakfast table. "Dear Brennan, I attended your parish renewal all this week. You are eloquent, brilliant, poetic, witty, aesthetic, and . . . inflated. Last night when you stood in the parish hall after the service ended, where was the love in your eyes for each of us in the midst of your glory? Why didn't you stoop down and hug those little children? Why didn't you kiss the old ladies on the cheek? Why didn't you look at us from the core of your being, depth meeting depth, love meeting love. Man, are you blind!" The letter was signed, "A mirror."

Obviously the person needed something that I didn't give. Under the circumstances, his or her expectations may have been unreasonable. But even when I am not tired, I realize that I don't love as much as I could or should or would. Often I will think of a thoughtful thing to say to a woman in a counseling session twenty minutes after she has walked out the door.

I will hear what a woman says and not what she means and wind up giving sage advice to a nonproblem. Distracted by a disturbing phone call, I left home to give a lecture to the inmates of Trenton State Penitentiary and began with the outrageous greeting: "Well, it's nice to see so many of you here."

And so it goes. Frequently not on top, in control, or as the Irish say "in fine form." This is part of our poverty as human beings. When we have self-acceptance without self-concern we simply express reality. To be human is to be poor. Our impoverished spirit gives us pause before deciding to become tyrants to ourselves.[6]

Should you ask the biblically poor woman to describe her prayer life, she might answer: "Most of the time, my prayer consists in experiencing the absence of God in the hope of communion." She is not richly endowed with mystical experiences. That is fine because it reflects the truth of her impoverished humanity.

Yet the experience of absence does not mean the absence of experience. For example, the soldier in combat who, during a lull in the battle, steals a glance at his wife's picture tucked in his helmet, is more present to her at that moment in her absence than he is to the rifle that is present in his hands. Likewise, the poor in spirit perceive that religious experience and mystical 'highs' are not the goal of authentic prayer, rather the goal is communion with God.

The Christian who is truly poor in spirit goes to worship on Sunday morning singing: "I am poor but I brought myself the best I could; I am yours, I am yours."

One of the great lights in the history of prayer, Teresa of Avila, tells this story in her book *The Way of Perfection*: "I know a nun who could not practice anything but vocal prayer. . . . She came to me in great distress saying she did not know how to practice mental prayer, meditation, centering prayer and that she could not contemplate but only say vocal prayers. She was quite an old woman and had lived an extremely good and religious life. I asked her what prayers she said, and from her reply I saw that in simply saying the Lord's Prayer over and over, she was experiencing pure contemplation, and the Lord was raising her to be with him in union. So I praised the Lord and envied her vocal prayer."

The prayer of the poor in spirit can simply be a single word: Abba. Yet that word can signify dynamic interaction. Imagine a little boy trying to help his father with some household work, or making his mother a gift. The help may be nothing more than getting in the way, and the gift may be totally useless, but the love behind it is simple and pure, and the loving response it evokes is virtually uncontrollable. I am sure it is this way between our Abba and us. At the deepest, simplest levels, we just want each other to be happy, to be pleased. Our sincere desire counts far more than any specific success or failure. Thus when we try to pray and cannot, or when we fail in a sincere attempt to be compassionate, God touches us tenderly in return.

In this sense, there is no such thing as *bad* prayer. A third characteristic of the tilted-halo gang is honesty. We must know who we are. How difficult it is to be honest, to accept that I am unacceptable, to renounce self-justification, to give up the pretense that my prayers, spiritual insight, tithing, and successes in ministry have made me pleasing to God! No antecedent beauty enamors me in his eyes. I am lovable only because he loves me.

Honesty is such a precious commodity that it is seldom found in the world or the church. Honesty requires the truthfulness to admit the attachment and addictions that control our attention, dominate our consciousness, and function as false gods. I can be addicted to vodka or to being nice, to marijuana or being loved, to cocaine or being right, to gambling or relationships, to golf or gossiping. Perhaps my addiction is food, performance, money, popularity, power, revenge, reading, television, tobacco, weight, or winning. When we give anything more priority than we give to God, we commit idolatry. Thus we all commit idolatry countless times every day.

Once we accept the gospel of grace and seek to shed defense mechanisms and subterfuges, honesty becomes both more difficult and more important. Now, honesty involves the willingness to face the truth of who we are, regardless of how threatening or unpleasant our perceptions may be. It means hanging in there with ourselves and with God, learning our mind tricks by experiencing how they defeat us, recognizing our avoidances, acknowledging our lapses, learning completely that we cannot handle it ourselves. This steady self-confrontation requires strength and courage. We cannot use failure as an excuse to quit trying.[7]

Without personal honesty I can easily construct an image of myself that is rather impressive. Complacency will then replace delight in God. Many of us do not want the truth about ourselves; we prefer to be reassured of our virtue, as illustrated by this vignette. One day a preacher said to a friend, "We have just had the greatest revival our church has experienced in many years."

"How many did you add to your church membership?"

"None. We lost five hundred."[8]

To be alive is to be broken. And to be broken is to stand in need of grace. Honesty keeps us in touch with our neediness and the truth that we are saved sinners. There is a beautiful transparency to honest disciples who never wear a false face and do not pretend to be anything but who they are.

When a man or woman is truly honest (not just working at it), it is virtually impossible to insult them personally. There is nothing there to insult. Those who were truly ready for the kingdom were just such people. Their inner poverty of spirit and rigorous honesty had set them free. They were people who had nothing to be proud of.

There was the sinful woman in the village who had kissed Jesus' feet. There was freedom in doing that. Despised as a prostitute, she had accepted the truth of her utter nothingness before the Lord. She had nothing to lose. She loved much because much had been forgiven her.

The so-called Good Thief was a terrorist who acknowledged he was receiving the just reward of his crimes. He also had nothing to be proud of.

The Good Samaritan, chosen as the model of Christian compassion, was despised as a heretic of mixed pagan and Jewish ancestry. He was so unclean already that, unlike the priest and Levite who passed by with their halos on tight, he could afford to express his love for the wounded man left for dead.

Getting honest with ourselves does not make us unacceptable to God. It does not distance us from God, but draws us to him—as nothing else can—and opens us anew to the flow of grace. While Jesus calls each of us to a more perfect life, we cannot achieve it on our own. To be alive is to be broken; to be broken is to stand in need of grace. It is only through grace that any of us could dare to hope that we could become more like Christ.

The saved sinner with the tilted halo has been converted from mistrust to trust, has arrived at an inner poverty of spirit, and lives as best he or she can in rigorous honesty with self, others, and God.

The question which the gospel of grace puts to us is simply this: Who shall separate you from the love of Christ? What are you afraid of?

Are you afraid that your weakness could separate you from the love of Christ? It can't.

Are you afraid that your inadequacies could separate you from the love of Christ? They can't.

Are you afraid that your inner poverty could separate you from the love of Christ? It can't.

Difficult marriage, loneliness, anxiety over the children's future? They can't.

Negative self-image? It can't.

Economic hardship, racial hatred, street crime? They can't.

Rejection by loved ones or the suffering of loved ones? They can't.

Persecution by authorities, going to jail? They can't.

Nuclear war? It can't.

Mistakes, fears, uncertainties? They can't.

The gospel of grace calls out: Nothing can ever separate you from the love of God made visible in Christ Jesus our Lord.

You must be convinced of this, trust it, and never forget to remember. Everything else will pass away, but the love of Christ is the same yesterday, today, and forever. Faith will become vision, hope will become possession, but the love of Jesus Christ that is stronger than death endures forever. In the end, it is the one thing you can hang onto.

Chapter 5

Cormorants and Kittiwakes

Several years before his death, a remarkable rabbi, Abraham Joshua Heschel, suffered a near-fatal heart attack. His closest male friend was at his bedside. Heschel was so weak he was only able to whisper: "Sam, I feel only gratitude for my life, for every moment I have lived. I am ready to go. I have seen so many miracles during my lifetime." The old rabbi was exhausted by his effort to speak. After a long pause, he said, "Sam, never once in my life did I ask God for success or wisdom or power or fame. I asked for wonder, and he gave it to me."

I asked for wonder, and he gave it to me. A Philistine will stand before a Claude Monet painting and pick his nose; a person filled with wonder will stand there fighting back the tears.

By and large, our world has lost its sense of wonder. We have grown up. We no longer catch our breath at the sight of a rainbow or the scent of a rose, as we once did. We have grown bigger and everything else smaller, less impressive. We get blasé and worldly wise and sophisticated. We no longer run our fingers through water, no longer shout at the stars or make faces at the moon. Water is H_2O, the stars have been classified, and the moon is not made of green cheese. Thanks to satellite TV and jet planes, we can visit places available in the past only to a Columbus, a Balboa, and other daring explorers.

There was a time in the not too distant past when a thunderstorm caused grown men to shudder and feel small. But God is being edged out of his world by science. The more we know about meteorology, the less inclined we are to pray during a thunderstorm. Airplanes now fly above, below, and around them. Satellites reduce them to photographs. What ignominy—if a thunderstorm could experience ignominy! Reduced from theophany to nuisance!

Heschel says that today we believe all enigmas can be solved, and all wonder is nothing but "the effect of novelty upon ignorance." Certainly, the new can amaze us: a space shuttle, the latest computer game, the softest diaper. Till tomorrow, till the new becomes old, till yesterday's wonder is discarded or taken for granted. Small wonder Rabbi Heschel concluded, "As civilization advances, the sense of wonder declines."

We get so preoccupied with ourselves, the words we speak, the plans and projects we conceive that we become immune to the glory of creation. We barely notice the cloud passing over the moon or the dewdrops clinging to the rose leaves. The ice on the pond comes and goes. The wild blackberries ripen and wither. The blackbird nests outside our bedroom window. We don't see her. We avoid the cold and the heat. We refrigerate ourselves in summer and entomb ourselves in plastic in winter. We rake up every leaf as fast as it falls. We are so accustomed to buying prepackaged meats and fish and fowl in supermarkets we never think and blink about the bounty of God's creation. We grow complacent and lead practical lives. We miss the experience of awe, reverence, and wonder.[1]

Our world is saturated with grace, and the lurking presence of God is revealed not only in spirit but in matter—in a deer leaping across a meadow, in the flight of an eagle, in fire and water, in a rainbow after a summer storm, in a gentle doe streaking through a forest, in Beethoven's Ninth Symphony, in a child licking a chocolate ice cream cone, in a woman with windblown hair. God intended for us to discover his loving presence in the world around us.

For several centuries the Celtic Church of Ireland was spared the Greek dualism of matter and spirit. They regarded the world with the clear vision of faith. When a young Celtic monk saw his cat catch a salmon swimming in shallow water, he cried, "The power of the Lord is in the paw of the cat." The Celtic chronicles tell of the wandering sailor monks of the Atlantic, seeing the angels of God and hearing their song as they rose and fell over the western islands. To the scientific person they were only gulls and gannets, puffins, cormorants and kittiwakes. But the monks lived in a world in which everything was a word of God to them, in which the love of God was manifest to anyone with the least creative imagination. How else, they wondered, would God speak to them? They cherished the Scriptures but they also cherished God's ongoing revelation in his world of grace. "Nature breaks through the eyes of a cat," they said.[2] For the eyes of faith, every created thing manifests the grace and providence of Abba.

So often we religious people walk amid the beauty and bounty of nature and we talk nonstop. We miss the panorama of color and sound and smell. We might as well have remained inside in our closed, artificially lit living rooms. Nature's lessons are lost and the opportunity to be wrapped in silent wonder before the God of creation passes. We fail to be stretched by the magnificence of the world saturated with grace. Creation doesn't calm our troubled spirits, restore our perspective, or delight us in every part of our being.[3] It reminds us instead of mundane chores: changing the page on the calendar or ordering our snow tires. We must rediscover the gospel of grace and the world of grace.

For "the grace of our Lord Jesus Christ, the love of God and the fellowship of the Holy Spirit" opens us to the divine spread everywhere about us, especially in the life of a loving person.

I am thinking of the beggar in Molière's *Don Juan*. He sits at the corner of the street as a nobleman passes. The passing stranger is the aristocrat Don Juan, an embittered man, both his fortune and his character ruined.

"An alms for the love of God," cries the beggar.

Don Juan stops, reaches in his pocket and holds out his last gold coin above the outstretched arms of the beggar. "Blaspheme God, and I'll give it to you."

"O no, my Lord," says the beggar, "I would never do that." A gesture like that is more grace-full than a heaven full of stars, a thousand symphonies, an Eiffel Tower, or a Mona Lisa. Thomas Aquinas said that the splendor of a soul in grace is so seductive that it surpasses the beauty of all created things.

A story is told about Fiorello LaGuardia, who, when he was mayor of New York City during the worst days of the Great Depression and all of World War II, was called by adoring New Yorkers 'the Little Flower' because he was only five foot four and always wore a carnation in his lapel. He was a colorful character who used to ride the New York City fire trucks, raid speakeasies with the police department, take entire orphanages to baseball games, and whenever the New York newspapers were on strike, he would go on the radio and read the Sunday funnies to the kids.

One bitterly cold night in January of 1935, the mayor turned up at a night court that served the poorest ward of the city. LaGuardia dismissed the judge for the evening and took over the bench himself. Within a few minutes, a tattered old woman was brought before him, charged with stealing a loaf of bread. She told LaGuardia that her daughter's husband had deserted her, her daughter was sick, and her two grandchildren were starving. But the shopkeeper, from whom the bread was stolen, refused to drop the charges. "It's a bad neighborhood, your Honor," the man told the mayor. "She's got to be punished to teach other people around here a lesson."

LaGuardia sighed. He turned to the woman and said "I've got to punish you. The law makes no exceptions—ten dollars or ten days in jail." But even as he pronounced sentence, the mayor was already reaching into his pocket. He extracted a bill and tossed it into his famous sombrero saying: "Here is the ten dollar fine which I now remit; and furthermore I am going to fine everyone in this courtroom fifty cents for living in a town where a person has to steal bread so that her grandchildren can eat. Mr. Bailiff, collect the fines and give them to the defendant."

So the following day the New York City newspapers reported that $47.50 was turned over to a bewildered old lady who had stolen a loaf of bread to feed her starving grandchildren, fifty cents of that amount being contributed by the red-faced grocery store owner, while some seventy petty criminals, people with traffic violations, and New York City policemen, each of whom had just paid fifty cents for the privilege of doing so, gave the mayor a standing ovation.[4]

What an extraordinary moment of grace for anyone present in that courtroom! The grace of God operates at a profound level in the life of a loving person. Oh, that we would recognize God's grace when it comes to us!

Recently I directed a three-day silent retreat for six women in Virginia Beach. As the retreat opened, I met briefly with each woman and asked them to write on a sheet of paper the one grace that they would most like to receive from the Lord. A married woman from North Carolina, about forty-five years old, with an impressive track record of prayer and service to others, told me she wanted more than anything to actually experience just one time the love of God. I assured her that I would join her in that prayer.

The following morning this woman (whom I'll call Winky) arose before dawn and went for a walk on the beach which was less than fifty yards from our house. Walking along the seashore barefoot, with the chilly waters of the Atlantic Ocean lapping up against her feet and ankles, she noticed some one hundred yards away a teen-age boy and a woman some fifteen yards behind walking in her direction. In less than a minute the boy had passed by to her left but the woman made an abrupt ninety-degree turn, walked straight toward Winky, embraced her deeply, kissed her on the cheek, whispered "I love you" and continued on her way. Winky had never seen the woman before. Winky wandered along the beach for another hour before returning to the house. She knocked on my door. When I opened it, she was smiling. "Our prayer was answered," she said simply.

In his book, *The Magnificent Defeat*, Frederick Buechner writes: "For what we need to know, of course, is not just that God exists, not just that beyond the steely brightness of the stars there is a cosmic intelligence of some kind that keeps the whole show going, but that there is a God right here in the thick of our day-by-day lives who may not be writing messages about himself in the stars but in one way or another is trying to get messages through our blindness as we move around down here knee-deep in the fragrant muck and misery and marvel of the world. It is not objective proof of God's existence that we want but the experience of God's presence. That is the miracle we are really after, and that is also, I think, the miracle that we really get."[5]

Living by the gospel of grace leads us into what Teilhard de Chardin called, 'the divine milieu'—a

God-filled, Christ-soaked universe, a world charged with the grandeur of God. How do we live in the presence of the living God? In wonder, amazed by the traces of God all around us.

Grace abounds in contemporary movies, books, novels, films, and music. If God is not in the whirl wind, he may be in a Woody Allen film or a Bruce Springsteen concert. Most people understand imagery and symbol better than doctrine and dogma. Images touch hearts and awaken imaginations. One theologian suggested that Springsteen's "Tunnel of Love" album, in which he symbolically sings of sin, death, despair, and redemption, is more important for Catholics than the Pope's last visit when he spoke of morality only in doctrinal propositions. Troubadours have always been more important and influential than theologians and bishops.

Elsewhere in the media, a modern version of the medieval morality play has slipped into prime time television almost without anyone noticing it. In many ways Bill Cosby is the most influential religion teacher in America.

Every week his program presents vivid and appealing paradigms of love to vast audiences. This love is disclosed by the resolution of family tensions in the lives of characters who have become as real to us as your next door neighbors—Cliff, Claire, Sondra, Denise, Theo, Vanessa, Rudi and so on. We learn, without even realizing it, how to live lovingly in families. We laugh at the familiar pattern of conflict and tension created by apparently trivial family crises like an engagement announcement, a fiftieth birthday, a big telephone bill, a fight between young lovers, a wedding anniversary of grandparents, a divorce between friends, an assault of the flu on the family. As we laugh, we see the virtues required for conflict resolution like patience, trust, sensitivity, honesty, flexibility, and forgiveness.[6]

Family life has been the raw material of much of Cosby's humor from the beginning of his career, and it has always been a humor of love. Perhaps his doctorate in education has made him more reflective about what he is doing, more conscious of the moral and spiritual issues he is tackling, but he has always been, in his own way, a vehicle of grace.

Grace makes a striking breakthrough in a novel called *The Moviegoer* by the Southern writer Walker Percy. He tells the story of a commuter on the way home from his successful job, a man who inexplicably feels bad in proportion to the many reasons he has to feel good. Suddenly he suffers a severe heart attack and is removed from the train at a station he has passed countless times before but never visited. When the commuter regains consciousness, he is in a strange hospital bed surrounded by unfamiliar people. As his eye wanders around the room, he catches sight of the hand spread out on the sheet in front of him. It is as if he had never seen his own hand until this moment— this extraordinary thing able to move this way and that—to open and close.

Percy goes on to speak about this awakening as a revelation, an experience of what theologians would call 'natural grace'. Through the heart attack the commuter was able to encounter himself and his life in a way he had not for years, absorbed as he was in what he calls "everydayness." The ordeal restored him to himself. The event is of enormous existential importance, for what he chooses to do with the experience will be the whole burden of his future. When he rode the train every day, he was gripped by a nameless despair. Now the catastrophe of the heart attack has liberated him from the paralysis of a living death and launched him on a search for meaning.[7]

In the hospital he keeps staring at his hand. The commuter says, "My hand was open in front of my face. The fingers closed and opened. I felt like Rip Van Winkle waking up and testing his bones. Was anything broken? Was I still in one piece?"

"Like Rip Van Winkle waking up." Percy presents the catastrophe as a rough shaking out of sleep, a blast of cold air, or, as the Moviegoer puts it, "a good kick in the ass." It is only the reality of death that is powerful enough to quicken people out of the sluggishness of everyday life and into an active search for what life is really about. Percy plunges his heroes into disaster and ordeal, only to speak out of the whirlwind about the worst of times being the best of times, about the preferability of hurricanes over good weather, about the willing return of soldiers to their worst nightmares. Percy's people not only live through the catastrophe but discover in it the freedom to act and to be. The commuter grabs his own existence round the neck and begins to live a renewed life in an ordinary world that had not been cleansed of "everydayness."

Our gracious God speaks to us in this novel and issues a call "to choose between generativity and stagnation, between continuing to have an impact, or sitting around waiting to die." It is the language of grace, conversion, *metanoia*, put in contemporary terms since, as Percy says, the old words of grace have been devalued.

Was it this novel that inspired Erma Bombeck to write a column entitled "If I Had My Life to Live Over Again"? In it, she wrote:

I would have invited friends over to dinner even if the carpet was stained and the sofa faded. I would have sat on the lawn with my children and not worried about grass stains. I would never have bought anything just because it was practical, wouldn't show soil or was guaranteed to last a lifetime. When my child kissed me impetuously, I would never have said, "Later. Now get washed up for dinner." There would have been more I love yous, more I'm sorrys, but mostly, given another shot at life, I would seize every minute, look at it and really see it, live it, and never give it back.

Once again, right in the middle of our daily newspaper, an echo of grace. Each moment of our existence, we are either growing into more or retreating into less. We are either living a little more or dying a little bit, as Norman Mailer put it.

The spirituality of wonder knows the world is charged with grace, that while sin and war, disease and death are terribly real, God's loving presence and power in our midst are even more real.

In the grasp of wonder, I am surprised, I'm enraptured. It's Moses before the burning bush "afraid to look at God" (Exodus 3:6). It's Stephen about to be stoned: "I see the Son of Man standing at God's right hand" (Acts 7:56), and Michelangelo striking his sculptured Moses and commanding him "Speak!" It's Ignatius of Loyola in ecstasy as he eyes the sky at night, Teresa of Avila ravished by a rose. It's doubting Thomas discovering his God in the wounds of Jesus, Mother Teresa spying the face of Christ in the tortured poor It's America thrilling to footsteps on the moon, a child casting his kite to the wind. It's a mother looking with love at her newborn infant. It's the wonder of a first kiss.[8]

The gospel of grace is brutally devaluated when Christians maintain that the transcendent God can only be properly honored and respected by denying the goodness and the truth and the beauty of the things of this world.

Amazement and rapture should be our reaction to the God revealed as Love.

For a moment allow me to sketch with broad strokes a biblical theology of divine agapé.

Israel's earliest concept of God was based on the covenant, the contract made on Mt. Sinai. Through their spokesman, Moses, God said to the Israelites: "You will be my people, and I shall be your God." Yahweh is first perceived by the Jewish community as a personal, relating Being. Their concept of God was vastly superior to that of the pagans whose gods were quite human, fickle, capricious, erotic, as unpredictable as the forces with which they were identified—wind, storm, fertility, the nation, and so forth.

Israel knew a holy God, transcending everything visible and tangible, yet personal. He was somehow reflected in things but was not to be identified with things. Exodus depicts God as stable, interested, a Rock of dependability among so many dependents.

Thus the Jews related to a covenant-God who had initiated the contract, who had talked to Israel first, begotten her as a people, and given her a sense of identity. In this primitive stage of the relationship, Israel's God was calm, even cold. The qualities of interest, fidelity, and stability were appreciated, but warmth and radiance had not yet appeared. Yahweh was like the Rock of Gibralter in the wind of changing events. He had a face but it was deadpan with a touch of benignity: reminiscent of Charlton Heston or Matt Dillon, there was no sugar or fancy to Yahweh. He was firm, just, a basis for confidence: he was easily diverted from walking a straight line down Main Street or pursuing a kidnapped child across the desert and through Indian country right into the heart of Mexico. Unrelenting dependability. Israel's election was utterly gratuitous. No need for Nell to wear make-up or fancy finery like the other seductive belles. Matt Dillon is not seduced. He chooses Nell freely, homely as she was, and that gave her a real sense of confidence. It was a little scary at times, even a bit unreal and inhuman.

Israel's concept of God needed clearer definition, for God is not inhuman but will wear humanity, as he ultimately does in Jesus, far beyond the limits of humanity as we know it, so that he can be everything we are and are not.

Now God raised up the prophets, burned into their consciousness a lively awareness of his presence, and sent them to reveal him in a warmer, more passionate manner. Though Israel had played the prostitute whoring after false gods, the prophets cry the constancy of God in the face of human infidelity: "Israel, don't ever be so foolish as to measure my love for you in terms of your love for me! Don't ever compare your thin, pallid, wavering, and moody love with my love, for I am God, not man."

Human love will always be a faint shadow of God's love. Not because it is too sugary or sentimental but simply because it can never compare from whence it comes. Human love with all its passion and emotion is a thin echo of the passion/emotion love of Yahweh.

In the Sinai wilderness the covenant-God was faithful and just. Israel was faithful. They were related. But if Israel became unfaithful, logic and human justice required no further pursuit of Yahweh. He sees the contract broken, picks up his briefcase, and walks out of court. The relationship is ended.

But we cannot apply human logic and justice to the living God. Human logic is based on human experience and human nature. Yahweh does not conform to this model. If Israel is unfaithful, God remains faithful against all logic and all limits of justice because *he is*. Love clarifies the happy irrationality of God's conduct. Love tends to be irrational at times. It pursues despite infidelity. It blossoms into jealousy and anger—which betrays keen interest. The more complex and emotional the image of God becomes in the Bible, the bigger he grows, and the more we approach the mystery of his indefinability.

The hesed of Yahweh draws Israel into greater confidence. Justice says: "I owe you nothing, for you have broken the contract." But where justice ends, love begins, and reveals that God is not interested merely in the dividends of the covenant. He is looking into the eyes of Israel from his depths to hers. He sees through the smokescreen of deeds good and bad to Israel herself. She glances up uneasily, "Who? Me?"

"Yes, you. I don't want the abstractions of relationship. I want your heart." (This is not the tone of contemporary spirituality. Many of us put God on Pier 40 as a niggling customs officer. He rifles through our moral suitcase to sort out our deeds, and then hands us a scorecard to tally up virtues and vices, so we can match baseball cards with him on Judgment Day.)

According to Hosea, God is willing to maintain a relationship even when his spouse has become a coarse and vulgar prostitute. This same conviction is carried into the New Testament. The adulterous woman is brought before Jesus. The god of religious leaders, who never got over Hosea's contribution, is expected to judge her. She has been unfaithful and the divine posture embodied in leadership would stone her. The God of the Pharisees is interested in the contract, in justice first and foremost. Let us kill the woman for the contract. The person is expendable.

But in the man, Jesus, we see the human face of God, one in keeping with Old Testament revelation. He is interested in the woman. His love moves beyond justice and proves more salvific than spelling out the ground rules all over again.[9]

Unjust? To our way of thinking, yes. Thank God! I am wonderfully content with a God who doesn't deal with me as my sins deserve. On the last day when Jesus calls me by name, "Come, Brennan, blessed of my Father," it will not be because Abba is just, but because his name is mercy.

Will we ever understand the gospel of grace, the furious love of God, the world of grace in which we live? Jesus Christ is the scandal of God. When the Baptizer is imprisoned by Herod, he sends a couple of his followers to ask Jesus: "Are you the One who is to come into the world or should we wait for another?" Jesus says, "Go back and tell John what you have seen and heard: the blind see, the deaf hear, the lame walk, the poor have the gospel preached to them, the messianic era has erupted into history, and the love of my Father is revealed. Blessed is he who is not *scandalized* in me."

We should be astonished at the goodness of God, stunned that he should bother to call us by name, our mouths wide open at his love, bewildered that at this very moment we are standing on holy ground.

Every parable of mercy in the gospel was addressed by Jesus to his opponents: murmuring scribes, grumbling Pharisees, critical theologians, members of the Sanhedrin. They are the enemies of the gospel of grace, indignant because Jesus asserts that God cares about sinners, incensed that he should eat with people they despised. What does he tell them?

These sinners, these people you despise are nearer to God than you. It is not the hookers and thieves who find it most difficult to repent: it is you who are so secure in your piety and pretense that you have no need of conversion. They may have disobeyed God's call, their professions have debased them, but they have shown sorrow and repentance. But more than any of that, these are the people who appreciate his goodness: they are parading into the kingdom before you: for they have what you lack—a deep gratitude for God's love and deep wonder at his mercy.

Let us ask God for the gift he gave to an unforgettable rabbi, Joshua Abraham Heschel: "Dear Lord, grant me the grace of wonder. Surprise me, amaze me, awe me in every crevice of your universe. Delight me to see how your Christ plays in ten thousand places, lovely in limbs, and lovely in eyes not his, to the Father through the features of men's faces. Each day enrapture me with your marvelous things without number. I do not ask to see the reason for it all; I ask only to share the wonder of it all."

Chapter 6

Grazie, Signore

In his book *Mortal Lessons*, Richard Selzer, M.D., writes: "I stand by the bed where a young woman lies, her face postoperative, her mouth twisted in palsy, clownish. A tiny twig of the facial nerve, the one to the muscles of her mouth, has been severed. She will be thus from now on. The surgeon had followed with religious fervor the curve of her flesh; I promise you that. Nevertheless, to remove the tumor in her cheek, I had to cut the little nerve.

"Her young husband is in the room. He stands on the opposite side of the bed and together they seem to dwell in the evening lamplight, isolated from me, private. Who are they, I ask myself, he and this wry mouth I have made, who gaze at and touch each other so generously, greedily? The young woman speaks.

"Will my mouth always be like this?" she asks.

"Yes," I say, "it will. It is because the nerve was cut."

She nods and is silent. But the young man smiles. "I like it," he says, "It is kind of cute."

"All at once I *know* who he is. I understand and I lower my gaze. One is not bold in an encounter with a god. Unmindful, he bends to kiss her crooked mouth and I am so close I can see how he twists his own lips to accommodate to hers, to show her that their kiss still works."[1]

Since reading this passage, the image of the husband contorting his mouth and twisting his lips for an intimate kiss with his palsied wife haunted me. Yet something eluded me until one day in prayer, it exploded anew in my memory of the violence on a hill outside the city wall of old Jerusalem. The mangled body of the Son hangs exposed to the world's derision. He is a blasphemer of God and a seducer of the people. Let him die in disgrace. His friends are scattered, his honor broken, his name a laughingstock. He has been forsaken by his God. Left absolutely alone. Drive him out of the holy city and across the tracks where his kind belong. The ragamuffin Christ is roughly handled, pushed around, scourged and spat upon, murdered and buried among his own ilk.

In order to dramatize his death, some Christian artists have given the crucified Christ a rolling eye and a contorted mouth; they use red lead to make realistic drops of blood flow from his hands, feet, and side.

In 1963 a friend gave me an expensive crucifix. A French artist had carved in wood, carved very delicately, the hands of Jesus on the cross. On Good Friday the Roman artists carved—O God, how they carved!—our brother Jesus with no trouble at all. No art was needed to bang in the nails with hammers, no red lead to make real blood gush from his hands, feet, and side. His mouth was contorted and his lips twisted simply by hoisting him up on the crossbeam. We have so theologized the passion and death of this sacred man that we no longer see the slow unraveling of his tissue, the spread of gangrene, his raging thirst.

In his monumental work, *The Crucified God*, Jurgen Moltmann writes: "We have made the bitterness of the cross, the revelation of God in the cross of Jesus Christ, tolerable to ourselves by learning to understand it as a necessity for the process of salvation."[2]

Roslyn and I stroll down Royal Street in the French Quarter in New Orleans. Adjacent to the infamous Bourbon Street with its jazz emporiums, T-shirt stores, and sex boutiques, Royal is studded with antique shops. "Come look at this," says the antique dealer. "The Venus costs more, but this ivory Christ crucified is beautiful in its own way, especially against a black velvet backdrop." And the more we reproduce him, the more we forget about him and the agony of his third hour. We turn him into gold, silver, ivory, marble or whatever to free ourselves from his agony and death as a man.

"For our sake God made the sinless one into sin, so that in him we might become the goodness of God" (2 Corinthians 5:21). Every form of sin and its consequences, sickness and disease of every kind, drug addiction, alcoholism, broken relationships, insecurity, hatred, lust, pride, envy, jealousy, cancer, bone disease, arthritis, and on and on were experienced and carried by "a thing despised and rejected by men" (Isaiah 53:3) who knew the nadir of an agony such as no one has ever dreamed. "In other words, God in Christ was reconciling the world to himself, not holding men's faults against them, and he has entrusted to us the good news that they are reconciled" (2 Corinthians 5:19). Jesus Christ nailed to the wood has carried our pain into the peace of grace. He has made peace through the blood of his cross (Colossians 1:20).

Jesus has journeyed to the far reaches of loneliness. In his broken body he has carried your sins and mine, every separation and loss, every heart broken, every wound of the spirit that refuses to close, all the riven experiences of men, women, and children across the bands of time.

Jesus is God. You and I were fashioned from the clay of the earth and the kiss of his mouth.

What shall we say to such an outpouring of love? How shall we respond?

First, the love of Christ and his gospel of grace calls for a personal, free, and unconventional decision. To respond is to acknowledge that the other has taken the initiative and issued the invitation. The other's overture has made a response necessary.

However, the other is not some itinerant salesperson at the door peddling bric-a-brac. It is Christ offering the opportunity of a lifetime: "I, the Light, have come into the world, so that whoever believes in me need not stay in the dark anymore" (John 12:46).

There is an extraordinary power in storytelling that stirs the imagination and makes an indelible impression on the mind. Jesus employs a set of stories, known as the 'crisis' parables to issue a warning, a summons to repentance, because of the lateness of the hour. Jesus says, "A tidal wave is approaching and you are lollygagging on the patio having a party." Or as Joachim Jeremias puts it, "You are feasting and dancing—on the volcano which may erupt at any moment."[3] The impending crisis precludes procrastination. "Stay awake, because you do not know when the master of the house is coming, evening, midnight, cockcrow, dawn; if he comes unexpectedly, he must not find you asleep. And what I say to you, I say to all: 'Stay awake!' "

In the parable of the wedding feast, the guest without a wedding garment is forcibly seized by the bouncers and heaved out the door. "The festal garment is repentance. Put it on today before your death, the day before the Deluge breaks, put it on today! The demand of the crisis is conversion."[4]

Rome is burning, Jesus says. Drop your fiddle, change your life, and come to me. When a tornado comes tearing down the street, it is not time to stop and smell the flowers. Let go of the good old days that never were—a regimented church you never attended, traditional virtues you never practiced, legalistic obedience you never honored, and a sterile orthodoxy you never accepted. The old era is done. The decisive inbreak of God has happened.

The person who realizes the gravity of the situation knows that the decision brooks no delay. The Storyteller calls us not to fear but to action. Don't cling to cheap, painted fragments of glass when the pearl of great price is being offered. When a person's very existence is threatened, when he or she stands on the threshold of moral ruin, when everything is at stake, the hour has struck for bold and resolute decision making.

In the parable of the talents, the three servants are called to render an account of how they have used the gifts entrusted to them. The first two used their talents boldly and resourcefully. The third, who prudently wraps his money and buries it, typifies the Christian who deposits his faith in an hermetic container and seals the lid shut. He or she limps through life on childhood memories of Sunday school and resolutely refuses the challenge of growth and spiritual maturity. Unwilling to take risks, this person loses the talent entrusted to him or her. "The master wanted his servants to take risks. He wanted them to gamble with his money."[5]

In a parable that was patently provocative to his Jewish audience, Jesus told the story of the crafty steward. We are presented with an embezzler who, to cover his tracks, launders his employer's money by falsifying his accounts. And Jesus praises the criminal!

"There was a rich man and he had a steward who was denounced to him for being wasteful with his property. He called for the man and said, 'What is this I hear about you? Draw me an account of your stewardship because you are not to be my steward any longer.' Then the steward said to himself, 'Now that my master is taking the stewardship from me, what am I to do? Dig? I am not strong enough. Go begging? I should be too ashamed. Ah, I know what I will do to make sure that when I am dismissed from office, there will be some to welcome me into their homes.'

"Then he called his master's debtors one by one. To the first he said, 'How much do you owe my master?' 'One hundred measures of oil' was the reply. The steward said, 'Here, take your bond, sit down straight away and write fifty.' To another he said, 'And you, sir, how much do you owe?' 'One hundred measures of wheat' was the reply. The steward said, 'Here take your bond and write eighty.'

"The master praised the dishonest steward for his astuteness. 'For the children of this world are more astute in dealing with their own kind than are the children of light' " (Luke 16:1-8).

Men and women whose outlook on life is conditioned by the Dow are shrewder on the street than are the disciples on their spiritual journey. Unbelievers put us to shame. Imitate their shrewdness!

Jesus did not excuse the steward's action but admired his initiative. He did not let a tragic sequence of events unfold but did what he had to do, however unscrupulously, to make a new life for himself. Without illusions, he makes the most of the little time that remains. "The unjust steward who, hearing he is going to be fired, doctors his master's accounts to secure another job, is commended precisely because he acted. The point does not concern morality but apathy. Here is a man who finds himself in a crisis and instead of wallowing in self-pity, acts resourcefully. The guests who do not respond to the King's banquet are quickly rejected and others are summoned. *Immediate response is the mood of the kingdom.* Imaginative shock issues an invitation which leads to decision and action."[6]

Most of us postpone a decision hoping that Jesus will get weary of waiting and the inner voice of Truth will get laryngitis. Thus, the summons of the 'crisis' parables remains suspended in a state of anxiety, so long as we opt neither for nor against the new dimension of living open to us. Our indecision creates more problems than it solves. Indecision means we stop growing for an indeterminate length of time; we get stuck. With the paralysis of analysis, the human spirit begins to shrivel. The conscious awareness of our resistance to grace and the refusal to allow God's love to make us who we really are brings a sense of oppression. Our lives become fragmented, inconsistent, lacking in harmony and out of sync. The worm turns. The felt security of staying in a familiar place vanishes. We are caught between a rock and hard place. How do we resolve this conundrum?

We don't.

We cannot will ourselves to accept grace. There are no magic words, preset formulas, or esoteric rites of passage. Only Jesus Christ sets us free from indecision. The Scriptures offer no other basis for conversion than the personal magnetism of the Master.

One morning, mysteriously moved by grace, a young man decides to try prayer. For five minutes he agrees to show up and shut up. And Jesus whispers: "Now is the time! The unreal world of glasnost and Gucci loafers, Häagen-Dazs Ice Cream and Calvin Klein jeans, beaver vests, Persian rugs, silk underwear, and the Super Bowl is passing away. *Now* is the time to stop running around frantically like Lancelot's horse in four directions at once and quietly remember that only one thing is necessary. Now is the time for personal decision and creative response to my word.

"Let me tell you a little story. One year a rich fool had a bonanza crop and made provisions for an even bigger one the following year. He said to himself, 'You're a good ole boy. You've worked hard, deserve everything that's coming to you, and have a nest egg for the future. Take it easy, eat heartily, drink up a storm, and have a good time.'

"That night my Father shattered his security. 'Fool! This very night the demand will be made for your soul; and this hoard of yours, who is going to enjoy it now?' "

In prayer Jesus slows us down, teaches us to count how few days we have, and gifts us with wisdom. He reveals to us that we are so caught up in what is urgent that we have overlooked what is essential. He ends our indecision and liberates us from the oppression of false deadlines and myopic vision.

Second, our response to the love of Jesus demands trust. Do we rely on our résumé or the gospel of grace? How do we cope with failure? "Grace tells us that we are accepted just as we are. We may not be the kind of people we want to be, we may be a long way from our goals, we may have more failures than achievements, we may not be wealthy or powerful or spiritual, we may not even be happy, but we are nonetheless accepted by God, held in his hands. Such is his promise to us in Jesus Christ, a promise we can trust."[7]

For those who feel their lives are a grave disappointment to God, it requires enormous trust and reckless, raging confidence to accept that the love of Christ knows no shadow of alteration or change. When Jesus said, "Come to me, all you who labor and are heavy burdened," he assumed we would grow weary, discouraged, and disheartened along the way. These

words are a touching testimony to the genuine human-
ness of Jesus. He had no romantic notion of the cost of
discipleship. He knew that following him was as
unsentimental as duty, as demanding as love. He knew
that physical pain, the loss of loved ones, failure, loneliness, rejection, abandonment, and betrayal would sap
our spirits; that the day would come when faith would
no longer offer any drive, reassurance, or comfort; that
prayer would lack any sense of reality or progress; that
we would echo the cry of Teresa of Avila: "Lord, if this
is the way you treat your friends, no wonder you have
so few!"

"For it is not as if we had a high priest who was
incapable of feeling our weaknesses with us; but we
have one who has been tempted in every way that we
are, though he was without sin. Let us be confident,
then, in approaching the throne of grace, that we shall
have mercy from him and find grace when we are in
need of help" (Hebrews 4:15-16).

A poet has written: "The desire to feel loved is
the last illusion: let it go and you will be free." Just as
the sunrise of faith requires the sunset of our former
unbelief, so the dawn of trust requires letting go of our
craving spiritual consolations and tangible reassurances. Trust at the mercy of the response it receives is
a bogus trust. All is uncertainty and anxiety. In trem-
bling insecurity the disciple pleads for proofs from the
Lord that her affection is returned. If she does not
receive them, she is frustrated and starts to suspect that
her relationship with Jesus is all over or that it never
even existed.

If she does receive consolation, she is reassured
but only for a time. She presses for further proofs—

each one less convincing than the one that went before. In the end the need to trust dies of pure frustration. What the disciple has not learned is that tangible reassurances, however valuable they may be, cannot create trust, sustain it, or guarantee any certainty of its presence. Jesus calls us to hand over our autonomous self in unshaken confidence. When the craving for reassurances is stifled, trust happens.

The mystery of Jesus' ascension into heaven contains an important lesson. He said to his disciples: "I must tell you the truth: it is for your own good that I am going" (John 16:7). Why? How could Jesus' departure profit the apostles? Because while he was still visible on earth, there was the danger they would be too wedded to the sight of his flesh, that they would leave the certainty of faith and lean upon the tangible evidence of the senses. To see Jesus in the flesh was good but "more blessed are they who have not seen and have believed" (John 20:29).

When we wallow in guilt, remorse, and shame over real or imagined sins of the past we are disdaining God's gift of grace.

Preoccupation with self is always a major component of unhealthy guilt and recrimination. It stirs our emotions, churning in self-destructive ways, closes us in upon the mighty citadel of self, leads to depression and despair and preempts the presence of a compassionate God. The language of unhealthy guilt is harsh. It is demanding, abusing, criticizing, rejecting, accusing, blaming, condemning, reproaching, and scolding. It is one of impatience and chastisement. Christians are shocked and horrified because they have failed. Unhealthy guilt becomes bigger than life. The image of the childhood story "Chicken Little" comes to mind. Guilt becomes the experience in which people feel the sky is falling.

Yes, we feel guilt over sins, but healthy guilt is one which acknowledges the wrong done and feels remorse, but then is free to embrace the forgiveness that has been offered. Healthy guilt focuses on the realization that all has been forgiven, the wrong has been redeemed.

"We all have shadows and skeletons in our backgrounds. But listen, there is something bigger in this world than we are and that something bigger is full of grace and mercy, patience and ingenuity. The moment the focus of your life shifts from your badness to his goodness and the question becomes not 'What have I done?' but 'What can he do?' release from remorse can happen; miracle of miracles, you can forgive yourself because you are forgiven, accept yourself because you are accepted, and begin to start building up the very places you once tore down. There is grace to help in every time of trouble. That grace is the secret to being able to forgive ourselves. Trust it."[8]

Perhaps you've heard this story: Four years ago in a large city in the far West, rumors spread that a certain Catholic woman was having visions of Jesus. The reports reached the archbishop. He decided to check her out. There is always a fine line between the authentic mystic and the lunatic fringe.

"Is it true, m'am, that you have visions of Jesus?" asked the cleric.

"Yes," the woman replied simply.

"Well, the next time you have a vision, I want you

to ask Jesus to tell you the sins that I confessed in my last confession."

The woman was stunned. "Did I hear you right, bishop? You actually want me to ask Jesus to tell me the sins of your past?"

"Exactly. Please call me if anything happens."

Ten days later the woman notified her spiritual leader of a recent apparition. "Please come," she said.

Within the hour the archbishop arrived. He trusted eye-to-eye contact. "You just told me on the telephone that you actually had a vision of Jesus. Did you do what I asked?"

"Yes, bishop, I asked Jesus to tell me the sins you confessed in your last confession."

The bishop leaned forward with anticipation. His eyes narrowed.

"What did Jesus say?"

She took his hand and gazed deep into his eyes. "Bishop," she said, "these are his exact words: 'I CAN'T REMEMBER.' "

Christianity happens when men and women accept with unwavering trust that their sins have not only been forgiven but forgotten, washed away in the blood of the Lamb. Thus, my friend archbishop Joe Reia says, "A sad Christian is a phony Christian and a guilty Christian is no Christian at all."

The conversion from mistrust to trust is wrought at the foot of the cross. "Upon the Calvary of Christ's death the saints meditate, contemplate, and experience their Lord."[9] There is an essential connection between experiencing God, loving God, and trusting God. You will trust God only as much as you love him. And you will love him to the extent you have touched him, rather that he has touched you.

Several years ago an anxious, fearful man in his mid-thirties came to a retreat I preached. A group of men who had known him for several years were on the same retreat and were astounded by the way they saw him change. Even his facial expression was transformed. Suddenly he had become free to trust. The basic experience was the deep realization that God loved him. It occurred through prayer. He was deeply moved by the words of Paul: "What proves that God loves us is that Christ died for us while we were still sinners" (Romans 5:8). His experience of human love had not the power to free him from mistrust as did that simple prayer before the crucified Christ.

The cross is a confrontation with the overwhelming goodness of God revealed in the broken body of his only begotten Son. Our personal encounter, not simply the intellectual cognition, but the experiential awareness of the love of Jesus Christ, propels us to trust. More than three hundred years ago, Claude de la Columbiere, commenting on the dinner Jesus attended in the home of Simon the Pharisee, wrote: "It is certain that of all those present, the one who most honors the Lord is Magdalene who is so persuaded of the infinite mercy of God that all her sins appear to her as but an atom in the presence of this mercy."

The prophetic word spoken by Jesus to a thirty-four-year-old widow, Marjory Kempe, in Lynn, Massachusetts, in 1667 remains ever ancient, ever new: "More pleasing to me than all your prayers, works, and penances is that you would believe I love you."

The grace to let go and let God be God flows from trust in his boundless love. "Since God did not spare his own Son, but gave him up to benefit us all, we may be certain, after such a gift, that he will not refuse us anything he can give" (Romans 8:32). Yet, many of us find it exceedingly difficult to trust. Perhaps haunted by the specter of parents who lived in poverty, indoctrinated by slogans like: "In God we trust; everybody else pays cash," and songs such as "Jesus saves his money at the Chase Manhattan Bank," we grew up with a skeptical spirit and assumed managerial control of our destiny.

Only love empowers the leap in trust, the courage to risk everything on Jesus, the readiness to move into the darkness guided only by a pillar of fire. Trust clings to the belief that whatever happens in our lives is designed to teach us holiness. The love of Christ inspires trust to thank God for the nagging headache, the arthritis that is so painful, the spiritual darkness that envelops us; to say with Job, "If we take happiness from God's hand, should we not take sorrow too?" (Job 2:10); to pray with Charles Foucauld: "Abba, I abandon myself into your hands. Do with me what you will. Whatever you may do, I thank you. I am ready for all: I accept all. Let your will be done in me and in all your creatures. I wish no more than this, O Lord. Into your hands I commend my spirit. I offer it to you with all the love of my heart, for I love you, Lord, and I give myself, surrender myself into your hands without reserve, with boundless confidence, *for you are my Father.*"

A Bahamian priest related a story that captures the essence of biblical trust. "A two-story house had caught on fire. The family—father, mother, several children—

were on their way out when the smallest boy became terrified, tore away from his mother, ran back upstairs. Suddenly he appeared at a smoke-filled window crying like crazy. His father, outside, shouted: 'Jump, son, jump! I'll catch you.' The boy cried: 'But, daddy, I can't see you.' 'I know,' his father called, 'I know. But I can see you.' "[10]

The third characteristic of our response to the gratuitous intervention of Jesus in our lives is heartfelt gratitude.

In O. Henry's famous short story "The Gift of the Magi," the young wife has only $1.87 to buy her husband a gift, and Christmas is the next day. Impulsively she decides to sell her long, thick hair to buy him a chain for this treasured gold watch. At the same moment he is selling the watch to buy his present for her—special combs for her beautiful hair.

Have you ever done such an extravagant thing spontaneously? Gone off and emptied the piggy bank because a certain gift was perfect for someone you cherished?

"Jesus was at Bethany in the house of Simon the leper; he was at dinner when a woman came in with an alabaster jar of *very costly* ointment, pure nard. She broke the jar and poured the ointment on his head. Some of those who were there said to one another indignantly, 'Why this waste of ointment? Ointment like this could have been sold for over three hundred denarii and the money given to the poor;' and they were angry with her. But Jesus said, 'Leave her alone. Why are you upsetting her? You have the poor with you always and you can be kind to them whenever you wish, but you will not always have me. She has done what was in her power to do; she has anointed my body beforehand for burial. I tell you solemnly, wherever throughout the world the Good News is proclaimed, what she has done will be told also, in remembrance of her' "(Mark 14:3-9).

What an impulsive, lovely gesture of gratitude! By human reckoning it was a foolish and wasteful thing to do. Yet Jesus was so deeply moved he wanted the tale of this woman's recklessness told and retold across the generations until the end of time.

Obviously, Jesus is saying there is a real place for the impulsive and spontaneous, the lavish and impractical, the heroic and extraordinary, the unrestrained and incalculable bursts of generosity that cry out: "It is right to give you thanks and praise." Yet, our gratitude to Jesus is for the most part our unsung service to those around us. "I tell you solemnly, insofar as you did this to one of the least of these brothers of mine, you did it to me" (Matthew 25:40).

Though Christ no longer visibly moves among us, we minister to him in the ragamuffins within reach. Each encounter with a brother or sister is a mysterious encounter with Jesus himself. In the upper room, the Man like us in all things but ungratefulness, spelled out the game plan of gratitude: "Love one another as I have loved you." To Peter on the beach along the Sea of Tiberias, "If you love me, Simon, Son of John, tend my sheep." Quite simply, our deep gratitude to Jesus Christ is manifested neither in being chaste, honest, sober and respectable, nor in church-going, Bible-toting and Psalm-singing, but in our deep and delicate respect for one another.

Even Sunday worship is subordinated to reconciliation with others. "If you are bringing your offering to the altar and there remember that your brother has something against you, leave your offering there before the altar, go and be reconciled with your brother first, and then come back and present your offering" (Matthew 5:23-24). Worship, cult, and religion in general have no absolute autonomy of their own for Jesus. God is a Being for others, not a Being for himself alone. "Cultic worship is not only hypocritical but absolutely meaningless if it is not accompanied by love for other people; for in such a way it cannot possibly be a way of giving thanks to God."[11]

The ministry of evangelization is an extraordinary opportunity of showing gratitude to Jesus by passing on his gospel of grace to others. However, the 'conversion by concussion' method with one sledge hammer blow of the Bible after another betrays a basic disrespect for the dignity of the other and is utterly alien to the gospel imperative to bear witness. To evangelize a person is to say to him or her: you, too, are loved by God in the Lord Jesus. And not only to say it but to really think it and relate it to the man or woman so they can sense it. This is what it means to announce the Good News. *But that becomes possible only by offering the person your friendship*, a friendship that is real, unselfish, without condescension, full of confidence, and profound esteem.

The movie *Amadeus* was a remarkable film centered on two powerful and contrasting figures, Salieri, the court composer to the Emperor, and Wolfgang Amadeus Mozart, the brash and conceited young genius. "Someone described his life as wine, women and song. And he didn't sing much."[12]

The limited, uninspired Salieri lives with a raging

jealousy for the limitless, God-given talent of Mozart. Yet, after every laborious score that he writes, Salieri whispers "Grazie, Signore"—Thank you, Lord. This song of Salieri lies at the heart of our response to the graciousness of God and the gospel of grace.

Grazie, Signore, for your lips twisted in love to accommodate my sinful self, for judging me not by my shabby good deeds but by your love that is your gift to me, for your unbearable forgiveness and infinite patience with me, for other people who have greater gifts than mine, and for the honesty to acknowledge that I am a ragamuffin. When the final curtain falls and you summon me home, may my last whispered word on earth be the wholehearted cry, "Grazie, Signore."

Chapter 7

Paste Jewelry and Sawdust Hot Dogs

Counterfeit grace is as commonplace as fake furs, phony antiques, paste jewelry, and sawdust hot dogs.

The temptation of the age is to look good without being good. If 'white lies' were criminal offenses, we would all be in jail by nightfall. It took a lot of cooperation to create the atmosphere wherein the Charlotte and Baton Rouge televangelist scandals finally blossomed. The dichotomy between what we say and what we do is so pervasive in the church and in society that we actually come to believe our illusions and rationalizations and clutch them to our hearts like favorite teddy bears.

The HUD disgrace that rocked the nation's capital last year caused Meg Greenfield to write in *Newsweek*:

"The particularly cynical feature of this case is that people who have made a career, and a pretty successful career at that, of inveighing against corruption, mismanagement and near-criminal incompetence that in fact do afflict some big government enterprises, have joined the opposition. The HUD scandal was particularly gross because it was an inside job and because it was so eminently a betrayal of the very values to which their administration claimed a unique loyalty."[1]

Impostors in the Spirit always prefer appearances to reality. Rationalization begins with a look in the mirror. We don't like the sight of ourselves as we really are, so we try cosmetics, makeup, the right light, and the proper accessories to develop an acceptable image of ourselves. We rely on the stylish disguise that has made us look good or at least look away from our true self. Self-deception mortgages our sinfulness and prevents us from seeing ourselves as we really are—ragamuffins.

One of my indelible memories goes back to April 1975 when I was a patient at an alcoholic rehabilitation center in a small town north of Minneapolis. The setting was a large, split-level recreation room on the brow of a hill overlooking an artificial lake. Twenty-five chemically dependent men were assembled. Our leader was a trained counselor, skilled therapist, and senior member of the staff. His name was Sean Murphy-O'Connor, though he normally announced his arrival with the statement: "It's himself. Let's get to work."

Sean directed a patient named Max to sit on "the hot seat" in the center of the U-shaped group. A small, diminutive man, Max was a nominal Christian, married with five children, owner and president of his company, wealthy, affable, and gifted with remarkable poise.

"How long have you been drinking like a pig, Max?" Murphy-O'Connor had begun the interrogation.

Max winced. "That's quite unfair."

"We shall see. I want to get into your drinking history. How much booze per day?"

Max relit his corncob pipe. "I have two Marys with the men before lunch and twin Martins after the office closes at five. Then . . ."

"What are Marys and Martins?" Murphy-O'Connor interrupts.

"Bloody Marys—Vodka, tomato juice, a dash of lemon and Worcestershire, a splash of Tabasco; and Martinis, Beefeaters gin, extra dry, straight up, ice cold with an olive and lemon twist."

"Thank you, Mary Martin. Continue."

"The wife likes a drink before dinner. I got her hooked on Martins several years ago. Of course she calls them 'pre-prandials.' " Max smiled. "Of course you understand the euphemism. Isn't that right, gentlemen?"

No. one responded.

"As I was saying, we have two martinis before dinner and two more before going to bed."

"A total of eight drinks a day, Max?" Murphy-O'Connor inquired.

"Absolutely right. Not a drop more, not a drop less."

"You're a liar!"

Unruffled, Max replied: "I'll pretend I didn't hear that. I have been in business for twenty-odd years and built my reputation on veracity not mendacity. People know my word is my bond."

"Ever hide a bottle in your house?" asked Benjamin, a Navajo Indian from New Mexico.

"Don't be ridiculous. I've got a bar in my living room as big as a horse's ass. Nothing personal, Mr. Murphy-O'Connor." Max felt he had regained control. He was smiling again.

"Do you keep any booze in the garage, Max?"

"Naturally. I have to replenish the stock. A man in my profession does a lot of entertaining at home." The executive swagger had returned.

"How many bottles in the garage?"

"I really don't know the actual count. Offhand, I would say two cases of Smirnoff Vodka, a case of Beefeater gin, a few bottles of bourbon and scotch, and a bevy of liquors."

The interrogation continued for another twenty minutes. Max fudged and hedged, minimized, rationalized, and justified his drinking pattern. Finally, hemmed in by relentless cross-examination, he admitted he kept a bottle of vodka in the night stand, a bottle of gin in the suitcase for travel purpose, another in his bathroom cabinet for medicinal purposes, and three more at the office for entertaining clients. He squirmed occasionally but never lost his veneer of confidence.

Max grinned. "Gentlemen, I guess we have all

gilded the lily once or twice in our lives," was the way he put it, implying that only men of large mien can afford the luxury of self-deprecating humor.

"You're a liar!" another voice boomed.

"No need to get vindictive, Charlie," Max shot back. "Remember the image in John's gospel about the speck in your brother's eye and the two-by-four in your own. And the other one in Matthew about the pot calling the kettle black."

(I felt constrained to inform Max that the speck and plank comparison were not found in John but in Matthew and the pot and the kettle was a secular proverb found in none of the gospels. But I sensed a spirit of smugness and an air of spiritual superiority had suddenly enveloped me like a thick fog. I decided to forego the opportunity for fraternal correction. After all, I was not at Hazelden doing research on a book. I was just another broken-down drunk like Max.)

"Get me a phone," said Murphy-O'Connor.

A telephone was wheeled into the room. Murphy-O'Connor consulted a memo pad and dialed a number in a distant city. It was Max's hometown. Our receiver was rigged electronically so that the party dialed could be heard loud and clear throughout the living room on the lake.

"Hank Shea?"

"Yeah, who's this?"

"My name is Sean Murphy-O'Connor. I am a counselor at an alcohol and drug rehabilitation center in the Midwest. Do you remember a customer named Max? (Pause) Good. With his family's permission I am researching his drinking history. You tend bar in that tavern every afternoon, so I am wondering if you could tell me approximately how much Max drinks each day?"

"I know Max well, but are you sure you have his permission to question me?"

"I have a signed affidavit. Shoot."

"He's a helluva guy. I really like him. He drops thirty bucks in here every afternoon. Max has his standard six martinis, buys a few drinks, and always leaves me a fin. Good man."

Max leapt to his feet. Raising his right hand defiantly, he unleashed a stream of profanity worthy of a stevedore. He attacked Murphy-O'Connor's ancestry, impugned Charlie's legitimacy and the whole unit's integrity. He clawed at the sofa and spat on the rug.

Then, in an incredible *coup de main* he immediately regained his composure. Max reseated himself and remarked matter-of-factly that even Jesus lost his temper in the temple when he saw the Sadducees hawking pigeons and pastries. After an extemporaneous homily to the group on justifiable anger, he stoved his pipe and presumed that the interrogation was over.

"Have you ever been unkind to one of your kids?" Fred asked.

"Glad you brought that up, Fred. I have a fantastic rapport with my four boys. Last Thanksgiving I took them on a fishing expedition to the Rockies. Four days of roughing it in the wilderness. A great time! Two of my sons graduated from Harvard, you know, and Max Jr. is in his third year at . . . "

"I didn't ask you that. At least once in his life every father has been unkind to one of his kids. I'm sixty-two years old and I can vouch for it. Now give us one specific example."

A long pause ensued. Finally, "Well, I was a little thoughtless with my nine-year-old daughter last Christmas Eve."

"What happened?"

"I don't remember. I just get this heavy feeling whenever I think about it."

"Where did it happen? What were the circumstances?"

"Wait one minute!" Max's voice rose in anger. "I told you I don't remember. Just can't shake this bad feeling."

Unobtrusively, Murphy-O'Connor dialed Max's hometown once more and spoke with his wife.

"Sean Murphy-O'Connor calling, ma'am. We are in the middle of a group therapy session, and your husband just told us that he was unkind to your daughter last Christmas Eve. Can you give me the details, please?"

A soft voice filled the room. "Yes, I can tell you the whole thing. It seems like it just happened yesterday. Our daughter Debbie wanted a pair of earth shoes for her Christmas present. On the afternoon of December 24, my husband drove her downtown, gave her sixty dollars, and told her to buy the best pair of shoes in the store. That is exactly what she did. When she climbed back into the pickup truck her father was driving, she kissed him on the cheek and told him he was the best daddy in the whole world. Max was preening himself like a peacock and decided to celebrate on the way home. He stopped at the Cork 'n'

Bottle—that's a tavern a few miles from our house— and told Debbie he would be right out. It was a clear and extremely cold day, about twelve degrees above zero, so Max left the motor running and locked both doors from the outside so no one could get in. It was a little after three in the afternoon and . . . "

Silence.

"Yes?"

The sound of heavy breathing crossed the recreation room. Her voice grew faint. She was crying. "My husband met some old Army buddies in the tavern. Swept up in euphoria over the reunion, he lost track of time, purpose, and everything else. He came out of the Cork 'n' Bottle at midnight. He was drunk. The motor had stopped running and the car windows were frozen shut. Debbie was badly frostbitten on both ears and on her fingers. When we got her to the hospital, the doctors had to operate. They amputated the thumb and forefinger on her right hand. She will be deaf for the rest of her life."

Max appeared to be having a coronary. He struggled to his feet making jerky, uncoordinated movements. His glasses flew to the right and his pipe to the left. He collapsed on all fours and sobbed hysterically.

Murphy-O'Connor stood up and said softly, "Let's split."

Twenty-four recovering alcoholics and addicts climbed the eight-step stairwell. We turned left, gathered along the railing on the upper split level and looked down. No man will ever forget what he saw that day, the twenty-fourth of April at exactly high noon. Max was still in the doggie position. His sobs had soared to shrieks. Murphy-O'Connor approached him, pressed his foot against Max's rib cage and pushed. Max rolled over on his back.

"You unspeakable slime," Murphy-O'Connor roared. "There's the door on your right and the window on your left. Take whichever is fastest. Get out of here before I throw up. I am not running a rehab for liars!"

The philosophy of tough love is based on the conviction that no effective recovery can be initiated until a man admits that he is powerless over alcohol and that his life has become unmanageable. The alternative to confronting the truth is always some form of self-destruction. For Max there were three options: eventual insanity, premature death, or sobriety. In order to free the captive, one must name the captivity. Max's denial had to be identified through merciless interaction with his peers. His self-deception had to be unmasked in its absurdity.

Later that same day Max pleaded for and obtained permission to continue treatment. He proceeded to undergo the most striking personality change I have ever witnessed. He got honest and became more open, sincere, vulnerable, and affectionate than any man in the group. Tough love had made him real and the truth had set him free.

The denouement to his story: The night before Max completed treatment, Fred passed by his room. The door was ajar. Max was sitting at his desk reading a novel entitled *Watership Down*. Fred knocked and entered. For several moments Max sat staring at the book. When he looked up, his cheeks were streaked with tears. "Fred," he said hoarsely, "I just prayed for the first time in my life." Max was on the road to knowing God.

An intimate connection exists between the quest for honesty and a transparent personality. Max could not encounter the truth of the living God until he faced his alcoholism. From a biblical perspective, Max was a liar. In philosophy, the opposite of truth is error: in Scripture, the opposite of truth is a lie. Max's lie consisted in appearing to be something he wasn't—a social drinker. Truth for him meant acknowledging reality—his alcoholic drinking.

The Evil One is the great illusionist. He varnishes the truth and encourages dishonesty. "If we say we have no sin in us, we are deceiving ourselves and refusing to admit the truth" (1 John 1:8). Satan prompts us to give importance to what has no importance. He clothes trivia with glitter and seduces us away from what is real. He causes us to live in a world of delusion, unreality, and shadows.

Jean Danielou wrote: "Truth consists in the mind giving to things the importance they have in reality." The really Real is God. When Max confronted and accepted the truth of his alcoholism, he stepped through a doorway into the acknowledgment of God's sovereign reality and claimed, "I just prayed for the first time in my life."

The noonday devil of the Christian life is the temptation to lose the inner self while preserving the shell of edifying behavior. Suddenly I discover that I am ministering to AIDS victims to enhance my résumé. I find I renounced ice cream for Lent to lose five excess pounds. I drop hints about the absolute priority of meditation and contemplation to create the impression that I am a man of prayer. At some unremembered moment I have lost the connection between internal purity of heart and external works of piety. In the most humiliating sense of the word, I have become a legalist. I have fallen victim to what T.S. Eliot calls the greatest sin: to do the right thing for the wrong reason.

"Beware of the scribes . . . these are the men who swallow the property of widows, while making a show of lengthy prayers" (Mark 12:38, 40). Jesus did not have a naive outlook on prayer. He knew it could be counterfeited by spiritual narcissism, hypocrisy, wordiness, and sensationalism. The noonday devil is not intimidated by the boundaries of time.

The letter of James counsels: Confess your sins to one another (James 5:16). This salutary practice aims to guide us in accepting ownership of our ragamuffin status, but as Dietrich Bonhoeffer noted, "He who is alone with his sins is utterly alone. It may be that Christians, not withstanding corporate worship, common prayer, and all their fellowship in service, may still be left to their loneliness. The final breakthrough to fellowship does not occur because, though they have fellowship with one another as believers and as devout people, they do not have fellowship as the undevout, as sinners. The pious fellowship permits no one to be a sinner. So everyone must conceal his sin from himself and from their fellowship. We dare not be sinners. Many Christians are unthinkably horrified when a real sinner is suddenly discovered among the righteous. So we remain alone with our sin, living in lies and hypocrisy. The fact is that we are sinners!"[2]

At Sunday worship, as in every dimension of our existence, many of us *pretend to believe* we are sinners. Consequently, all we can do is pretend to believe we have been forgiven. As a result, our whole spiritual life is pseudo-repentance and pseudo-bliss.

The appeal of paste jewelry and sawdust hot dogs is powerful. A small investment in apparent propriety and good deeds yields the rewards of the faith community—adulation and praise. Coupled with a charismatic personality and an attractive appearance, hypocrisy can earn a $640,000 apartment at Trump Towers, a $90,000 diamond ring from Tiffany's, and frequent flights on the Concordes to Europe.

The spiritual future of ragamuffins consists not in disavowing that we are sinners but in accepting that truth with growing clarity, rejoicing in God's incredible longing to rescue us in spite of everything. C.S. Lewis wrote: "It may be that salvation consists not in the canceling of these eternal moments but in the perfected humility that bears the shame forever, rejoicing in the occasion which is furnished to God's compassion and glad that it should be common knowledge to the universe. Perhaps in that eternal moment St. Peter—he will forgive me if I am wrong—forever denies his Master. If so, it would indeed be true that the joys of heaven are for most of us, in our present condition, an acquired taste—and certain ways of life may render the taste impossible of acquisition. Perhaps the lost are those who dare not go to such a public place."[3]

Biblically, there is nothing more detestable than a self-righteous disciple. He is so swollen with conceit that his mere presence is unbearable. However, a nagging question arises. Have I so insulated myself in a fortified city of rationalizations that I cannot see that I may not be as different from the self-righteous as I would like to think?

The following scenario plays in my imagination:

A humble woman seeks me out because of my vaunted reputation as a spiritual guide. She is simple and direct:

"Please teach me how to pray."

Tersely, I inquire, "Tell me about your prayer life."

She lowers her eyes and says contritely, "There's not much to tell. I say grace before meals."

Haughtily, I reply, "You say grace before meals! Isn't that nice, Madam. I say grace upon waking and before retiring, and grace again before reading the newspaper and turning on the television. I say grace before ambulating and meditating, before the theater and the opera, before jogging, swimming, biking, dining, lecturing, and writing. I even say grace before I say grace."

That night, soggy with self-approval, I go before the Lord. And he whispers, "You ungrateful turd. Even the desire to say grace is itself my gift."

There is an ancient Christian legend that goes this way: "When the son of God was nailed to the cross and gave up his spirit, he went straight down to hell from the cross and set free all the sinners who were there in torment. And the Devil wept and mourned for he thought he would get no more sinners for hell.

"Then God said to him, 'Do not weep, for I shall send you all those holy people who have become self-complacent in the consciousness of their goodness and self-righteous in their condemnation of sinners. And hell shall be filled up once more for generations until I come again.' "[4]

How long will it be before we discover we cannot dazzle God with our accomplishments?

When will we acknowledge that we need not and cannot buy God's favor?

When will we acknowledge that we don't have it all together and happily accept the gift of grace? When will we grasp the thrilling truth of Paul: "We acknowledge that what makes a man righteous is not obedience to the Law, but faith in Jesus Christ" (Galatians 2:16)?

Authentic faith leads us to treating others with unconditional seriousness and to a loving reverence for the mystery of the human personality. Authentic Christianity should lead to maturity, personality, and reality. It should fashion whole men and women living lives of love and communion.

False, manhandled religion produces the opposite effect. Whenever religion shows contempt or disregards the rights of persons, even under the noblest pretexts, it draws us away from reality and God. We can put 'reverse English' on religion and make religion an escape from religion.

John's gospel shows the religious leaders of Israel worried about Jesus.

"The chief priests and the Pharisees called a meeting. 'Here is this man working all these signs,' they said, 'and what action are we taking? If we let him go on in this way everybody will believe in him and the Romans will come and destroy the Holy Place and our nation.' One of them, Caiaphas, the high priest that year, said, 'You don't seem to have grasped the situation at all; you fail to see that it is better for one man to die for the people, than for the whole nation to be destroyed' " (John 11:47-50).

A terrible thing has happened to Caiaphas. Religion has left the realm of respect for person. For Caiaphas sacredness has become institutions, structures, and abstractions. He is dedicated to the people, so individual flesh and blood men are expendable. Caiaphas is dedicated to the nation. But the nation does not bleed like Jesus. Caiaphas is dedicated to the Temple—impersonal brick and mortar. Caiaphas became impersonal himself, no longer a warm human being but a robot, as fixed and rigid as his unchanging world.

The choice usually presented to Christians is not between Jesus and Barabbas. No one wants to appear an obvious murderer. The choice to be careful about is between Jesus and Caiaphas. And Caiaphas can fool us. He is a very 'religious' man.

The spirit of Caiaphas lives on in every century of religious bureaucrats who confidently condemn good people who have broken bad religious laws. Always for a good reason of course: for the good of the temple, for the good of the church. How many sincere people have been banished from the Christian community by religious power brokers as numb in spirit as Caiaphas!

The deadening spirit of hypocrisy lives on in prelates and politicians who want to look good but not be good; it lives on in people who prefer to surrender control of their souls to rules than run the risk of living in union with Jesus.

Eugene Kennedy writes: "The devil dwells in the urge to control rather than liberate the human soul. One can hardly live in these closing years of the twentieth century without realizing how the forces of control have gathered. . . . We stand by a dark forest through which fearful religious and political leaders would force us to pass in single file through their exclusive pathway of righteousness. They want to intimidate us, make us afraid and hand over our souls to them once more. Jesus saw such shadowed forces as the corrupters of the essential nature of religion in his time. They are no less so all these centuries later."[5]

The way we are with each other is the truest test of our faith. How I treat a brother or sister from day to day, how I react to the sin-scarred wino on the street, how I respond to interruptions from people I dislike, how I deal with normal people in their normal confusion on a normal day may be a better indication of my reverence for life than the anti-abortion sticker on the bumper of my car.

We are not pro-life simply because we are warding off death. We are pro-life to the extent that we are men and women for others, all others; to the extent that no human flesh is a stranger to us; to the extent that we can touch the hand of another in love; to the extent that for us there are no "others."

Today the danger of the pro-life position which I vigorously support is that it can be frighteningly selective. The rights of the unborn and the dignity of the age-worn are pieces of the same pro-life fabric. We weep at the unjustified destruction of the unborn. Did we also weep when the evening news reported from Arkansas that a black family had been shot-gunned out of a white neighborhood?

One morning I experienced a horrifying hour. I tried to remember how often between 1941 and 1988 I wept for a German or Japanese, a North Korean or North Vietnamese, a Sandinista or Cuban. I could not remember one. Then I wept, not for them, but for myself.

When we laud life and blast abortionists, our credibility as Christians is questionable. On one hand we proclaim the love and anguish, the pain and joy that goes into fashioning a single child. We proclaim how precious each life is to God and should be to us. On the other hand, when it is the enemy that shrieks to heaven with his flesh in flames, we do not weep, we are not shamed: we call for more.

The sensitive Jew remembers the Middle Ages: every ghetto structured by Christians; every forced baptism, every Good Friday program, every portrait of Shylock exacting his pound of flesh, every identifying dress or hat or badge, every death for conscience's sake, every back turned or shoulder shrugged, every sneer or slap or curse.[6]

With their tragic history as background, it is not surprising that many Jews are unimpressed with our anti-abortion stance and our arguments for the sacredness of human life. For they still hear cries of Christ-killer; the survivors of Auschwitz and Dachau still feel lashes on their backs; they still see images of human soap, still taste hunger, still smell gas. The history of Judaism is a story of caring: they are not sure we care for them.

The pro-life position is a seamless garment of reverence for the unborn and the age-worn, for the enemy, the Jew, and the quality of life of all people. Otherwise it is paste jewelry and sawdust hot dogs.

Relief comes from rigorous honesty with ourselves. It is interesting that whenever the evangelists Mark, Luke, or John mention the apostles, they call the author of the first gospel either Levi or Matthew. But in his own Gospel, he always refers to himself as 'Matthew the publican', never wanting to forget who he was and always wanting to remember how low Jesus stooped to pick him up.

We are publicans just like Matthew.

Honesty simply asks if we are open, willing, and able to acknowledge this truth. Honesty brings an end to pretense through a candid acknowledgment of our fragile humanity. It is always unpleasant, and usually painful, and that is why I am not very good at it. But to stand in the truth before God and one another has a unique reward. It is the reward which a sense of reality always brings. I know something extremely precious. I am in touch with myself as I am. My tendency to play the pseudo-messiah is torpedoed.

To the extent that I reject my ragamuffin identity, I turn away from God, the community, and myself. I become a man obsessed by illusion, a man of false power and fearful weakness, unable to think, act, or love.

Gerald May, a Christian psychiatrist in Washington D.C. writes: "Honesty before God requires the most fundamental risk of faith we can take: the risk that God is good, that God does love us unconditionally. It is in taking this risk that we rediscover our dignity. To bring the truth of ourselves, just as we are, to God, just as God is, is the most dignified thing we can do in this life."[7]

Lord Jesus, we are silly sheep who have dared to stand before you and try to bribe you with our preposterous portfolios. Suddenly we have come to our senses. We are sorry and ask you to forgive us. Give us the grace to admit we are ragamuffins, to embrace our brokenness, to celebrate your mercy when we are at our weakest, to rely on your mercy no matter what we may do. Dear Jesus, gift us to stop grandstanding and trying to get attention, to do the truth quietly without display, to let the dishonesties in our lives fade away, to accept our limitations, to cling to the gospel of grace, and to delight in your love. Amen.

Chapter 8

Freedom from Fear

In Dostoevsky's incomparable novel, *The Brothers Karamazov*, the charge flung by the Church—embodied in the Grand Inquisitor—against Jesus who has returned to earth is: "Why have you come to disturb us?"

After fifteen hundred years the institutional church, instead of proclaiming Jesus, had supplanted him. Ecclesiastical traditions and man-made laws had usurped Jesus, and the Church was living off the success of its ingenuity.

There was too much light and truth in Jesus. His word, "You will know the truth and the truth will make you free" was intolerable. The elders decided that men and women simply were not capable of being free; so the Church ascribed to itself the protection of souls entrusted to it, only to dispense it when absolutely necessary. Ordinary people could not endure the burden of freedom, so the Church took it away from them for their own good. They would only abuse and misuse it anyway. Delivered from the anxiety and torment of personal decision and responsibility, people would feel safe and happy in obedience to authority.

" 'They will be amazed at us,' says the Grand Inquisitor to Jesus, 'and will think of us as gods, because we, who set ourselves at their head, are ready to endure freedom, this freedom from which they shrink in horror; and because we are ready to rule over them—so terrible will it seem to them, in the end, to be free. But we shall say that we are obeying you and ruling only in your name. Again we shall be betraying them, for we shall not let you have anything to do with us anymore.' Indeed, 'Why have you come to disturb us?' The Grand Inquisitor means to take this Jesus who has come again, bringing freedom once again, and burn him at the stake in the name of the Church."[1]

The question had become not "What does Jesus say?" but "What does the church say?"* This question is still being asked today.

Sad but true: some Christians want to be slaves. It is easier to let others make decisions or to rely upon the letter of the law.

---

* This question was frequently posed to me by Catholics over my marriage in 1982. The law says an ordained priest cannot marry. While I disagree with the law, I vigorously defend the church's right to require mandatory celibacy for ordained clergy. With equal vigor, I reject the ecclesiastical verdict that Roslyn and I are living in adultery. Once again, a man-made law attempts to supersede divine law.

Raised from the dead, Jesus remains present in the community of disciples as the way to freedom. The Kingdom of God is a kingdom of freedom. Jesus invites and challenges us to enter this kingdom, to walk the royal road of freedom, to be set free by the Father's love. He calls ragamuffins everywhere to freedom from the fear of death, freedom from the fear of life, and freedom from anxiety over our salvation.

One of the loveliest lines I have ever read comes from Brother Roger, the Prior of the Protestant monks of Taize, France. "Assured of your salvation by the unique grace of our Lord Jesus Christ."[2] It is still difficult for me to read these words without tears filling my eyes. It is wonderful. Christ bore my sins, took my place, died for me, freed me from fear to walk the path of peace that leads to the Twelve Gates.

Sadly, many today are not experiencing what Paul calls in Romans 8:21, "the glorious freedom of the children of God." The basic problem was stated in the first chapter of this book: We accept grace in theory but deny it in practice. Living by grace rather than law leads us out of the house of fear into the house of love. "In love there can be no fear, but fear is driven out by perfect love: because to fear is to expect punishment, and anyone who is afraid is still imperfect in love" (1 John 4:18).

While we profess our faith in God's unconditional love, many of us still live in fear. Nouwen remarks: "Look at the many 'if' questions we raise: What am I going to do if I do not find a spouse, a house, a job, a friend, a benefactor? What am I going to do if they fire me, if I get sick, if an accident happens, if I lose my friends, if my marriage does not work out, if a war breaks out? What if tomorrow the weather is bad, the buses are on strike, or an earthquake happens? What if someone steals my money, breaks into my house, rapes my daughter, or kills me?"[3]

Once these questions guide our lives, we take out a second mortgage in the house of fear.

Jesus says simply, "Make your home in me, as I make mine in you" (John 15:4). Home is not a heavenly mansion in the afterlife but a safe place right in the midst of our anxious world. "If anyone loves me he will keep my word, and my Father will love him, and we shall come to him and make our home with him" (John 14:23).

Home is that sacred space—external or internal—where we don't have to be afraid; where we are confident of hospitality and love. In our society we have many homeless people sleeping not only on the streets, in shelters or in welfare hotels, but vagabonds who are in flight, who never come home to themselves. They seek a safe place through alcohol or drugs, or security in success, competence, friends, pleasure, notoriety, knowledge, or even a little religion. They have become strangers to themselves, people who have an address but are never at home, who never hear the voice of love or experience the freedom of God's children.

To those of us in flight, who are afraid to turn around lest we run into ourselves, Jesus says: "You have a home . . . I am your home . . . claim me as your home . . . you will find it to be the intimate place where I have found my home . . . it is right where you are . . . in your innermost being . . . in your heart."

The author of Hebrews describes Jesus as the one who has "set free all those who had been held in slavery all their lives by the fear of death" (Hebrews 2:15). The gospel of freedom proclaims that death is an illusion, a phantom, the bogeyman of little children: death is simply a transition into the one experience worthy of the name *life*.

Here is the root of Christian joy and mirth. It is why theologian Robert Hotchkins at the University of Chicago can insist: "Christians ought to be celebrating constantly. We ought to be preoccupied with parties, banquets, feasts, and merriment. We ought to give ourselves over to veritable orgies of joy because we have been liberated from the fear of life and the fear of death. We ought to attract people to the church quite literally by the fun there is in being a Christian." Unfortunately we sometimes become somber, serious, and pompous. We fly in the face of freedom and grimly dig deeper into the trenches. In the words of Teresa of Avila, "from silly devotions and sour-faced saints, spare us, O Lord."

Disgruntled and disgusted, The Prince of Darkness slinks up to the chalet of bummed-out disciples who have made their home in Jesus and nails a legal document to the door:

EVICTION NOTICE!

You are hereby banished from
the House of Fear forever.
With malice aforethought, you have
flagrantly withheld the monthly rent
Of guilt, anxiety, fear, shame
and self-condemnation.

You have adamantly refused to
worry about your salvation.

149

Already I overheard one dismal tenant say,
"There goes the neighborhood!"
Your freedom from fear is not only
dangerous but contagious.
Real estate values have plummeted;
gullible investors are hard to find.
Why?
Your callous and carefree rejection
of slavery!
A pox on you and
all deluded lovers of liberty!

The Prince

We must choose either Christ or the Law as author of salvation. Does freedom come through faith in Jesus or through obedience to the Torah? The issue is momentous. "When Christ freed us, he meant us to remain free. Stand firm, therefore, and do not submit again to the yoke of slavery" (Galatians 5:1). Jewish Christians were proclaiming that salvation was impossible without observance of the Mosaic Law. They promoted not simply supererogatory practices (acts beyond what faith calls for), but another gospel (1:6) which distorts the gospel of Christ (1:7).

Paul is livid in his epistle to the Galatians. "Are you people in Galatia mad?" (3:1). What hangs in the balance is the emancipation of Christianity. Paul is uncompromising: "We hold that faith in Christ rather than fidelity to the Law is what justifies us, and that no one can be justified by keeping the Law" (2:16). "The Law will not justify anyone in the sight of God, because we are told: the righteous man finds life through faith" (3:11). "Christ redeemed us from the curse of the Law by being cursed for our sake" (3:13).

Written in the heat of the moment, the letter is a flaming manifesto of Christian freedom. Christ's call on your lives is a call to liberty. Freedom is the cornerstone of Christianity. Would Paul be as apoplectic today at the goings-on in the American church? Would those still imprisoned in old guilts, crippled by fear, exhausted by scrupulosity, threatened by legalists and anxious over their salvation merit the same rebuke: "I am astonished by the promptness with which you have turned away from the one who called you and have decided to follow a different version of the Good News" (1:6)?

We have undoubtedly heard that freedom is not license for lust. Maybe that's all we've heard—what it isn't. "Such an approach, whatever its limited truth, is defensive and afraid. Those using it wish above all to warn us of the dangers of thinking about freedom, of yearning for freedom. Such an approach generally ends up by showing us, or at least attempting to show us, that freedom actually consists in following the law or in submitting to authority or in walking a well-trod path. Again, there may be some truth in these conclusions but there is lacking a sense of the dark side of law, and of authority, and of the well-trod path. Each may be and has been turned into an instrument of tyranny and human suffering."[4]

What does freedom in the Spirit look like? "Now the Lord is the Spirit, and where the Spirit of the Lord is, there is freedom" (2 Corinthians 3:17).

Freedom in Christ produces a healthy independence from peer pressure, people-pleasing, and the bondage of human respect. The tyranny of public opinion can manipulate our lives. What will the neighbors think? What will my friends think? What will people think? The expectations of others can exert a subtle but controlling pressure on our behavior.

As the chameleon changes colors with the seasons, so the Christian who wants to be well thought of by everyone attunes and adapts to each new personality and situation. Without a stable and enduring self-image a woman may offer radically different aspects of herself to different men: she may be pious with her pastor and seductive with the office manager. Depending upon company and circumstances, a man may be either a sweet-talking servant of God or a foul-mouthed, bottom-pinching boor. Continuity of character is conspicuously absent in both sexes.

"It seems only yesterday that we began to break out of our character armor," writes William Kilpatrick, "only a moment ago that we began to experiment with a wide range of possibilities, identities and relationships. Swings of the pendulum, however, take place rather rapidly these days . . . and already the pendulum of identity formation has taken an exaggerated swing toward fluidity and tentativeness and away from continuity and fidelity."[5]

In Christ Jesus freedom from fear empowers us to let go of the desire to appear good, so that we can move freely in the mystery of who we really are. Preoccupation with projecting the "nice guy" image, impressing newcomers with our experience, and relying heavily on the regard of others leads to self-consciousness, sticky pedestal behavior, and unfreedom in the iron grip of human respect. Unconsciously, we may clothe the Pharisee's prayer in the publican's formula. For most of us it takes a long time for the

Spirit of freedom to cleanse us of the subtle urges to be admired for our studied goodness. It requires a strong sense of our redeemed selves to pass up the opportunity to appear graceful and good to other persons.

Alms-giving affords such an opportunity, but the applause we hear will be payment in full for our generous offering. Self-consciousness, not virtue, is its own reward.

"But who can escape watching oneself do good in a world in which even the churches that worship Jesus have mastered the techniques of embarrassing people into charitable giving? How can free giving, blind as Justice balancing the scales, survive the pastor's printed list of donors, the intricacies of charity for tax purposes, booster ads and testimonial tickets wheedled out of us with the sly pressures of shame and guilt? Our fund-raising mechanisms are built on an appraisal of our motives that is as clear and uncluttered as that of Jesus; they are engineered to our hearts like bionic devices and they reveal a mixed rather than a totally crass picture of our impulses for giving."[6]

The account of the widow's mite suggests that all the best gifts come from the loving hearts of men and women who aren't trying to impress anybody, even themselves, and who have won freedom precisely because they have stopped trying to trap life into paying them back for the good they do.

I experienced a significant breakthrough into the freedom of the children of God at my first AA meeting. In the past I would have set great store not only on looking good but on thinking too often about who is looking. My self-image as a man of God and a disciplined disciple had to be protected at all costs. My ravenous insecurities made my sense of self-worth rise and fall like a sailboat on the winds of another's approval or disapproval. It was a supreme moment of liberation to stand up, kick the pedestal aside and simply state: "My name is Brennan; I am an alcoholic."

My spiritual director once told me, "Brennan, give up trying to look and sound like a saint. It will be a lot easier on everybody."

Living by grace inspires a growing consciousness that I am what I am in the sight of Jesus and nothing more. It is his approval that counts. Making our home in Jesus, as he makes his in us, leads to creative listening: "Has it crossed your mind that I am proud you accepted the gift of faith I offered you? Proud that you freely chose me, after I had chosen you, as your friend and Lord? Proud that with all your warts and wrinkles you haven't given up? Proud that you believe in me enough to try again and again?

"Are you aware how I appreciate you for wanting me? I want you to know how grateful I am when you pause to smile and comfort a child who has lost her way. I am grateful for the hours you devote to learning more about me; for the word of encouragement you passed on to your burnt-out pastor, for your visit to the shut-in, for your tears for the retarded. What you did to them, you did to me. Alas, I am sad when you do not believe that I have totally forgiven you or you feel uncomfortable approaching me."

Prayer is another area that many struggle with because they aren't aware that in the freedom of the Spirit there are as many ways of praying as there are individual believers. The cardinal rule in prayer remains the dictum of Don Chapman, "Pray as you can; don't pray as you can't."

Let us suppose you give your three-year-old daughter a coloring book and a box of crayons for her birthday. The following day, with the proud smile only a little one can muster, she presents her first pictures for inspection. She has colored the sun black, the grass purple, and the sky green. In the lower right-hand corner, she has added woozy wonders of floating slabs and hovering rings: on the left, a panoply of colorful, carefree squiggles. You marvel at her bold strokes and intuit that her psyche is railing against its own cosmic puniness in the face of a big, ugly world. Later at the office, you share with your staff your daughter's first artistic effort and you make veiled references to the early work of van Gogh.

A little child cannot do a bad coloring; nor can a child of God do bad prayer. "A father is delighted when his little one, leaving off her toys and friends, runs to him and climbs into his arms. As he holds his little one close to him, he cares little whether the child is looking around, her attention flitting from one thing to another, or just settling down to sleep. Essentially the child is choosing to be with her father, confident of the love, the care, the security that is hers in those arms. Our prayer is much like that. We settle down in our Father's arms, in his loving hands. Our mind, our thoughts, our imagination may flit about here and there; we might even fall asleep; but essentially we are choosing for this time to remain intimately with our Father, giving ourselves to him, receiving his love and care, letting him enjoy us as he will. It is very simple prayer. It is very childlike prayer. It is prayer that opens us out to all the delights of the kingdom."[7]

Jesus' tenderness is not in any way determined by how we pray or what we are or do. In order to free us for compassion toward others, Jesus calls us to accept his compassion in our own lives, to become gentle, caring, compassionate, and forgiving toward ourselves in our failure and need.

Compassion for others is not a simple virtue because it avoids snap judgments—right or wrong, good or bad, hero or villain: it seeks truth in all its complexity. Genuine compassion means that in empathizing with the failed plans and uncertain loves of the other person, we send out the vibration, "Yes, ragamuffin, I understand. I've been there too."

The story goes that a dynamic young business-woman showed signs of stress and strain. The doctor prescribed tranquilizers and asked her to report to him after a couple of weeks.

When she came back, he asked her if she felt any different. She said, "No, I don't. But I've observed that other people seem a lot more relaxed."

Usually we see other people not as they are, but as we are.[8]

A person, in a real sense, is what he or she sees. And seeing depends on our eyes. Jesus uses the metaphor of eyes more often than that of minds or wills. The old proverb, "The eyes are the windows of the soul," contains a profound truth. Our eyes reveal whether our souls are spacious or cramped, hospitable or critical, compassionate or judgmental. The way we see other people is usually the way we see ourselves. If we have made peace with our flawed humanity and embraced our ragamuffin identity, we are able to tolerate in others what was previously unacceptable in ourselves.

One night a seemingly self-absorbed young man arrived at the door to escort our daughter Simone on a date. While he waited in the den for Simone to complete her ablutions, he strutted in the den, affected several poses, muttered some monosyllabic inanities, obliquely studied himself in the mirror, yawned occasionally, and tried to exude a jaunty air of nonchalance. I asked myself, who is this young Turk?

Is he the narcissistic embodiment of smug fulfillment or a touching incarnation of the isolation and loneliness of young people who have been denied access to their own spiritual depths? Behind the mask of studied poses and minor vanities, was there a yearning awaiting redemption?

Judgment depends on what we see, how deeply we look at the other, how honestly we face ourselves, how willing we are to read the human story beneath the frightened face.

The gentleness of Jesus with sinners flowed from his ability to read their hearts. Behind people's grumpiest poses and most puzzling defense mechanisms, behind their arrogance and airs, behind their silence, sneers, and causes, Jesus saw little children who hadn't been loved enough and who had ceased growing because someone had ceased believing in them. His extraordinary sensitivity caused Jesus to speak of the faithful as children no matter how tall, rich, clever, and successful they might be.

"Assured of your salvation by the unique grace of our Lord Jesus Christ . . ." is the heartbeat of the gospel, joyful liberation from fear of the Final Outcome, a summons to self-acceptance, and freedom for a life of compassion toward others.

Obviously, we are not treating a trivial evangelical matter here. Compassionate love is the axis of the Christian moral revolution and the only sign ever given by Jesus by which a disciple would be recognized. "I give you a new commandment; love one another; just as I have loved you, you also must love one another. By this love you have for one another, everyone will know that you are my disciples" (John 13:34-35). The new commandment structures the new Covenant in the blood of Jesus. So central is the precept of fraternal love that Paul does not hesitate to call it the fulfillment of the entire law and the prophets (Romans 13:8-10).

Exaggeration and overstatement are not the danger here. The danger lurks in our subtle attempts to rationalize our moderation in this regard. Turning the other cheek, walking the extra mile, offering no resistance to injury, and forgiving seventy times seven are not whims of the Son of Man. "The only thing that matters is faith that makes its power felt through love" (Galatians 5:6).

"Reason demands moderation in love as in all things," writes John McKenzie, "but faith destroys moderation here. Faith tolerates a moderate love of one's fellow man no more than it tolerates a moderate love between God and man."[9]

Once again, gentleness toward ourselves constitutes the core of our gentleness with others. When the compassion of Christ is interiorized and appropriated to self ("The bruised reed he will not crush and the smoldering wick he will not quench" [Matthew 12:20]), the breakthrough into a compassionate stance toward others occurs. In a Catch-22 situation, the way of gentleness brings healing to ourselves and gentleness toward ourselves brings healing to others. Solidarity with ragamuffins frees the one who receives compassion and liberates the one who gives it in the conscious awareness "I am the other."

Certainly *tough love* and discipline have their place in the Christian family. If children are not educated to the difference between right and wrong, they can easily become neurotic. However, only the discipline administered out of love is corrective and productive. Discipline erupting from rage and vindictiveness is divisive in the family and counterproductive in the church. To present an ultimatum to an addicted teenager: "Seek treatment or split," is a loving and perhaps lifesaving response, as long as the clear distinction between the action and the agent is maintained. With great wisdom William Shakespeare wrote: "Sometimes 'tis necessary to be cruel in order to be kind."

Alcoholics Anonymous was founded on June 10, 1935, in Akron, Ohio, by Bill W. and Doctor Bob. In its early stages a lively debate arose over the qualifications for membership. Could certain individuals be excluded for whatever reason like some country clubs do? Who gets in and who gets left out? Who decided whether a particular alcoholic was deserving or undeserving? Some of the core group lobbied to limit membership to persons of moral responsibility; others insisted that the only dues were the simple admissions: "I think I'm an alcoholic. I want to stop drinking."

According to the *Twelve Steps and Twelve Traditions,* whose author naturally remains anonymous, the debate was resolved in a most unusual way. On the AA calendar it was Year Two. In that time nothing could be seen but two nameless, struggling groups of alcoholics trying to hold their faces up to the light.

A newcomer appeared at one of these groups, knocked on the door, and asked to be let in. He talked frankly with the groups oldest member and quickly established that he was a desperate case. Above all, he wanted to get well. "I must tell you that I am the victim of another addiction with a stigmatism even worse than alcoholism. You may not want me among you. Will you let me join your group or not?"

There was the dilemma. What should the group do? The oldest member summoned two others and, in confidence, laid the explosive facts on their laps. Said he, "Well, what about it? If we turn this man away, he'll soon die. If we let him in, only God knows what trouble he'll brew. What's your answer—yes or no?"

At first the elders could only look at the objections. "We deal with alcoholics only," they said. "Should we not sacrifice this one for the sake of the many?" So went the discussion while the newcomer's fate hung in the balance.

Then one of the three spoke in a very different tone. "What we are really afraid of," he said, "is our reputation. We are much more afraid of what people might say than the trouble this alcoholic might bring. As we've been talking, five short words have been running through my mind. Something keeps repeating to me, 'What would the Master do?' "

Not another word was said.

Let's return for a moment to *The Brothers Karamazov* which hurls a tremendous accusation against the Catholic Church. On innumerable occasions it has sinned against the freedom of the children of God, "but to be honest the accusation does not stand only against the Catholic Church. Or were not heretics and witches burnt at the stake in Calvin's and Luther's Churches too, and were not opponents fought with violence instead of compelled by love. Does not everything of which the Catholic Church is accused in the way of lack of freedom, arbitrariness, authoritarianism, and totalitarianism, exist in other shapes and forms, more or less disguised, among the Christians of other confessions, and indeed often more in small sects than in large churches?"[10]

Yet none of this is decisive. The decisive thing is the freedom of the Gospel of Jesus Christ. The ground and source of our freedom lies not in ourselves, who are by nature slaves to sin, *but in the freedom* of his grace setting us free in Christ by the Holy Spirit. We are free from the slavery of sin—for what? For the saving grace of the living God!

The Grand Inquisitor, an old man with withered face and sunken eyes, finally ended his blistering indictment against Jesus' naiveté and idealism. "When the Inquisitor ceased speaking, he waited some time for his Prisoner to answer him. His silence weighed down upon him. He saw that the Prisoner had listened intently all the time, looking gently in his face and evidently not wishing to reply. The old man longed for Him to say something, however bitter and terrible. But He suddenly approached the old man in silence and softly kissed him on his bloodless aged lips. That was all his answer. The old man shuddered. His lips moved. He went to the door, opened it, and said to Him, "Go . . . "[11]

And the kiss glowed in the old man's heart.

Chapter 9

The Second Call

Many people between the ages of thirty and sixty—whatever their stature in the community and whatever their personal achievements—undergo what can truly be called a second journey.

A man can have piled up an impressive portfolio of dollars and honors, get his name in *Who's Who*, and then wake up one morning asking, "Is it all worth it?" Competent teachers, nurses, and clergy can reach the top only to discover that the job no longer fascinates. There is nowhere higher to go. They find themselves terrified of stagnation and asking, "Should I switch careers? Would returning to school help?"

Gail Sheehy's second journey began at thirty-five when she was covering a story in northern Ireland.

She was standing next to a young man when a bullet blew off his face. On that Bloody Sunday in Londonderry, she felt herself confronted with death and with what she called "the arithmetic of life." She suddenly realized "No one is with me. No one keeps me safe. There is no one who won't ever leave me alone." Bloody Sunday threw Gail Sheehy off balance and flung at her a barrage of painful questions about her ultimate purpose and values.

It need not be a bullet that initiates a second journey. A thirty-five-year-old wife learns of her husband's infidelity. A forty-year-old company director finds that making money suddenly seems absurd. A forty-five-year-old journalist gets smashed up in a car accident. However it happens, such people feel confused and even lost. They can no longer keep life in working order. They are dragged away from chosen and cherished patterns to face strange crises. This is their second journey.[1]

Anne Tyler's heroine in her Pulitzer Prize-winning novel, *Breathing Lessons*, is driving along a country road with her husband at the wheel. Suddenly, this middle-aged woman cries out, "O Ira, what are we going to do with the rest of our lives?" This is the question of the second journey.

Second journeys usually end quietly with a new wisdom and a coming to a true sense of self that releases great power. The wisdom is that of an adult who has regained equilibrium, stabilized, and found fresh purpose and new dreams. It is a wisdom that gives some things up, lets some things die, and accepts human limitations. It is a wisdom that realizes: I cannot expect anyone to understand me fully. It is wisdom that admits the inevitability of old age and death.

It is a wisdom that has faced the pain caused by parents, spouse, family, friends, colleagues, business associates, and has truly forgiven them and acknowledged with unexpected compassion that these people are neither angels nor devils, but only human.

The second journey begins when we know we cannot live the afternoon of life according to the morning program. We are aware that we only have a limited amount of time left to accomplish that which is really important—and that awareness illumines for us what really matters, what really counts. This conviction provides a new center. We share the determination of John Henry Newman who, as his second journey comes to a close, heads home, sensing "I have a work to do in England."[2]

For the Christian, this second journey usually occurs between the ages of thirty and sixty and is often accompanied by a second call from the Lord Jesus. The second call invites us to serious reflection on the nature and quality of our faith in the gospel of grace, our hope in the new and not yet, and our love for God and people. The second call is a summons to a deeper, more mature commitment of faith where the naiveté, first fervor, and untested idealism of the morning and the first commitment have been seasoned with pain, rejection, failure, loneliness, and self-knowledge.

The call asks, do you really accept the message that God is head over heels in love with you? I believe that this question is at the core of our ability to mature and grow spiritually. If in our hearts we really don't believe that God loves us as we are, if we are still tainted by the lie that we can do something to make God love us more, we are rejecting the message of the cross.

What stands in the way of our embracing the second call? I can see three obstacles: a crisis of faith, of hope, and of love. Let me explain.

Imagine that Jesus is calling you today. He extends a second invitation—to accept his Father's love. And maybe you answer, "Oh, I know that. It's old hat. I've come to this book seeking an insight in a fit of fervor. I'm not red-hot, wide-open. I'll listen to anything you have to say, so go ahead, dazzle me. Lay a new word on me. I know the old one."

And God answers "That's what you don't know. You don't know how much I love you. The moment you think you understand is the moment you do not understand. I am God not man. You tell others about me—that I am a loving God. Your words are glib. My words are written in the blood of my only Son. The next time you preach about my love with such obnoxious familiarity, I may come and blow your whole prayer meeting apart. When you come at me with studied professionalism, I will expose you as a rank amateur. When you try to convince others that you understand what you are talking about, I will tell you to shut up and fall flat on your face. You claim you know I love you:

"Did you know that every time you tell me you love me, I say thank you?

"When your son comes to you asking, 'Do you like Susan more 'cause she skates better and she's a girl?' are you grieved and saddened over your child's lack of trust? Do you know that you do the same thing to me?

"Do you claim to know what we shared when Jesus withdrew to a deserted place or spent the night on a hillside alone with me? Do you know from where the inspiration to wash the feet of the twelve came? Do you understand that, motivated by love alone, your God became your slave in the Upper Room?

"Were you grieved by the divine command to Abraham that he slay his only begotten Isaac on Mount Moriah? Were you relieved when the angel intervened, Abraham's hand was stayed, and the sacrifice was not carried out? Have you forgotten that on Good Friday no angel intervened? That sacrifice was carried out, and it was my heart that was broken.

"Are you aware that I *had* to raise Jesus from the dead on Easter morning because my love is everlasting? Are you serenely confident that I will raise you too, my adopted child?"

Faith means you want God and want to want nothing else.

When God's love is taken for granted, we paint him into a corner and rob him of the opportunity to love us in a NEW AND SURPRISING way, and faith begins to shrivel and shrink. When I become so spiritually advanced that Abba is old hat, then the Father has been had, Jesus has been tamed, the Spirit has been corralled, and the Pentecostal fire has been extinguished. Evangelical faith is the antithesis of lukewarmness. It always means a profound dissatisfaction with our present state.

In faith there is movement and development. Each day something is new. To be Christian, *faith has to be new*, that is, alive and growing. It cannot be static, finished, settled. When Scripture, prayer, worship, ministry become routine, they are dead. When I conclude that I can now cope with the awful love of God, I have headed for the shallows to avoid the deeps. I could more easily contain Niagara Falls in a tea cup than I can comprehend the wild, uncontainable love of God.

If our faith is going to be criticized, let it be for the right reasons. Not because we are too emotional but because we are not emotional enough; not because our passions are so powerful but because they are so puny; not because we are too affectionate but because we lack a deep, passionate, uncompromising affection for Jesus Christ.

Several years ago I made a thirty-day silent retreat in the snow-covered hills of Pennsylvania. One word sounded and resounded in my heart throughout that month. Jesus did not say this on Calvary, though he could have, but he is saying it now: "I'm dying to be with you. *I'm really dying to be with you.*" It was as if he were calling to me for a second time. I realized that what I thought I knew was straw. I had scarcely glimpsed, I had never dreamed what his love could be. The Lord drove me deeper into solitude seeking not tongues, healing, prophecy, or a good religious experience each time I prayed, but *understanding* and the quest for pure, passionate Presence.

The second call is drawing us to a deeper faith. We need to ask ourselves: *Do I really believe the Good News of Jesus Christ?* Do I hear his word spoken to my heart: "Shalom, be at peace, I understand"? And what is my response to his second call, whispering to me,

"You have my love. You don't have to pay for it. You didn't earn it and can't deserve it. You only have to open to it and receive it. You only have to say yes to my love—a love beyond anything you can intellectualize or imagine"?

A second obstacle, closely related to a crisis in faith, is a crisis of hope. In Matthew 22, Jesus describes the Kingdom of God as a wedding feast. Do we really believe we are going into a wedding feast that has already begun? Are we optimistic about what will happen to us in this world, or are we fearful and pessimistic? Are we celebrating our union with the Bridegroom?

One evening last summer I was vacationing at the Jersey Shore. I took a walk around an artificial lake in Belmar. Across the lake was a banquet hall called the Barclay that hosted parties, conventions, wedding receptions, and so forth. Over a hundred people were filing in the front door. They had just come from a wedding at St. Rose Church and were going to the reception. It had already begun. They could hear the music and laughter, drinking, and dancing. And the looks on their faces! They were bursting with impatience, sure of their reserved seats, couldn't wait to get in. They looked like they were going to a festive celebration.

But most of us stand outside the banquet door listening to the merriment and festivity inside, half hoping that there really is a banquet in there and that it's the nature of the world to be a celebration. We'd like to go in and celebrate, but wow! What if it's wrong? What if there is no banquet in there? What if it's a trick?

Why don't a lot of us go in now? Because we know that inside it's not a perfect banquet for the simple fact that we are still living between the cross and the resurrection. Christianity doesn't deny the reality of suffering and evil. Remember after Jesus came down the mount of Transfiguration, he told his disciples that he was going up to Jerusalem—that he would be executed and that he would triumph over death. Jesus was not the least bit confident that he would be spared suffering. He knew that suffering was necessary. What he was confident of was vindication. Our hope, our acceptance of the invitation to the banquet, is not based on the idea that we are going to be free of pain and suffering. Rather it is based on the conviction that we will triumph over suffering.

Do you believe that you too will live? Because that's the meaning of Christian hope. It's not a pollyanna optimism. It's not something that yields to discouragement, defeat, and frustration. On the contrary Christian hope stands firm and serene, confident even in the face of the gas chamber, even in the face of terminal cancer. However serious we believe Good Friday is, we are confident that Easter Sunday lies ahead of us. And what if we do die? Jesus died too, and if Jesus died we believe that now he lives, and that we shall live too.

Or do we? Many lay people have remarked to me that from priests and ministers today they hear just about everything but proclamation of the Good News of the Kingdom. They hear about race, pollution, war, abortion, ecology, and a myriad other moral problems. None of them prevents proclamation, but not a single one of them is an adequate substitute for issuing invitations to the banquet. Are we hesitant to commit ourselves to the role of an eschatological herald because we're no longer sure that we believe in that role—another way of saying that we never really did believe it? Maybe we think such a role isn't relevant, that people won't take an eschatological herald seriously. To be really a disciple of Jesus one must be as committed to the message of the Kingdom as he was, and to preach it whether or not the audience finds it relevant.

This is the challenge inherent in the New Testament. If Jesus is to be believed, if his message is to be taken seriously, if God has indeed intervened with loving and saving mercy, then the message is supremely relevant and the issuance of invitations to the wedding banquet is supremely important. But the fundamental issue is not whether the world considers it relevant; it is whether it is true. And this can be decided only by a leap of commitment. One cannot be a disciple without being committed, and if there are many hesitant disciples today, the reason is that they have not yet made a decisive commitment.

This is what the second call of Jesus Christ means today: A summons to a new and more radical leap in hope, to an existential commitment to the Good News of the wedding feast.

If we believe in the exciting message of Jesus, if we hope in vindication, we must love, and even more, we must run the risk of being loved. Love is the third obstacle to our embracing the second call.

The idea that God is love is certainly not new with Jesus. In fact, it probably wasn't even exclusive to the Judeo-Christian tradition. Other men at other times in other parts of the world have thought or hoped or wished that the really REAL, the living God, might

171

actually love them. But Jesus added a note of confidence. He didn't say that maybe God was love, or that it would be nice if God were love. He said, GOD IS LOVE—*period.* But there is more to the message of Jesus. He insisted that his Father is crazy with love, that God is a kooky God who can scarcely bear to be without us. The parable that makes this truth so obvious is the prodigal son, the parable of the loving Father.

The emphasis is not on the sinfulness of the son but on the generosity of the Father. We ought to reread this parable periodically if only to catch the delicate nuance at the first meeting between the two. The son had his speech carefully rehearsed. It was an elegant, polished statement of sorrow. But the old man didn't let him finish. The son had barely arrived on the scene when suddenly, a fine new robe was thrown over his shoulders. He hears music, the fatted calf is being carried into the parlor, and he didn't even have a chance to say to his father, "I'm sorry."

God wants us back even more than we could possibly want to be back. We don't have to go into great detail about our sorrow. All we have to do, the parable says, is appear on the scene, and before we get a chance to run away again, the Father grabs us and pulls us into the banquet so we can't get away.

There is a fascinating passage in chapter 8 of John's Gospel about the woman caught in sin. Remember how the crowd dragged her before Jesus and asked, "What do we do about her? She was caught in adultery. Moses says we should stone her but the Romans won't let us stone people. What do you think?"

Jesus ignores them and begins to write in the sand. Then he looks up and says, "Well, let the one here who hasn't committed any sin throw the first rock." One by one they drift away. Then Jesus says to the woman: "Is there no one here to condemn you?" She says, "No one, Lord." He says "Okay, go, and don't commit this sin anymore."

Now, get the picture. Jesus didn't ask her if she was sorry. He didn't demand a firm purpose of amendment. He didn't seem too concerned that she might dash back into the arms of her lover. She just stood there and Jesus gave her absolution before she asked for it.

The nature of God's love for us is outrageous. Why doesn't this God of ours display some taste and discretion in dealing with us? Why doesn't he show more restraint? To be blunt about it, couldn't God arrange to have a little more dignity? Wow!

Now, if we were in his position, we'd know perfectly well how to behave—that prodigal son would have recited his speech down to the very last word. And when he got finished we would have said, "Well, you go away, prodigal son, and I'll think about this a couple of weeks. Then you'll be informed by parcel post whether I've decided to let you back on the farm or not."

I don't think anyone reading this would have approved of throwing rocks at the poor woman in adultery, but we would have made darn sure she presented a detailed act of contrition and was firm in her purpose of amendment. Because if we let her off without saying she was sorry, wouldn't she be back into adultery before sunset?

No, the love of our God isn't dignified at all, and apparently that's the way he expects our love to be. Not only does he require that we accept his inexplicable, embarrassing kind of love, but once we've accepted it, he expects us to behave the same way with others. I suppose I could live, if I had to, with a God whose love for us is embarrassing, but the thought that I've got to act that way with other people—that's a bit too much to swallow.

Perhaps the simplest, though certainly not the easiest place to start, is with myself. Carl Jung, the great psychiatrist, once reflected that we are all familiar with the words of Jesus, "Whatever you do to the least of my brethren, that you do unto me." Then Jung asks a probing question: "What if you discovered that the least of the brethren of Jesus, the one who needs your love the most, the one you can help the most by loving, the one to whom your love will be most meaningful—what if you discovered that this least of the brethren of Jesus . . . is *you?*"

Then do for yourself what you would do for others. And that wholesome self-love that Jesus enjoined when he said, "Love your neighbor as yourself" might begin with the simple acknowledgment, What is the story of my priesthood? It is the story of an unfaithful person through whom God continues to work! That word is not only consoling, it is freeing, especially for those of us caught up in the oppression of thinking that God can only work through saints. What a word of healing, forgiveness, and comfort it is for many of us Christians who have discovered that we are earthen vessels who fulfill Jesus' prophecy, "I tell you solemnly, this day, this night, before the cock crows twice, you will have disowned me three times"!

And the Lord is now calling me a second time, affirming me, enabling me, encouraging me, challenging me all the way into fullness of faith, hope, and love in the power of his Holy Spirit. Ignorant, weak, sinful person that I am, with easy rationalizations for my sinful behavior, I am being told anew in the unmistakable language of love, "I am with you, I am for you, I am in you. I expect more failure from you than you expect from yourself."

There is one barrier to love that deserves special mention because it is so crucial to the second call of Jesus Christ—fear. Most of us spend considerable time putting off the things we should be doing or we would like to do or we want to do—but are afraid to do. We are afraid of failure. We don't like it, we shun it, we avoid it because of our inordinate desire to be thought well of by others. So we come up with a thousand brilliant excuses for doing nothing. We put things off, waste the energies of life and love that are within us. And the judgment of the Lord High Executioner in the *Mikado* on the girl who perpetually procrastinated falls on us—"She'll never be missed; no, she'll never be missed!"

Each of us pays a heavy price for our fear of falling flat on our face. It assures the progressive narrowing of our personalities and prevents exploration and experimentation. As we get older we do only the things we do well. There is no growth in Christ Jesus without some difficulty and fumbling. If we are going to keep on growing, we must keep on risking failure throughout our lives. When Max Planck was awarded the Nobel prize for his discovery of quantum theory, he said, "Looking back over the long and labyrinthian path which finally led to the discovery, I am vividly reminded of Goethe's saying that men will always be making mistakes as long as they are striving after something."

You know, in spite of the fact that Christianity speaks of the cross, redemption, and sin, we're unwilling to admit failure in our life. Why? Partly because it's human nature's defense mechanism against its own inadequacies. But even more so, it's because of the successful image our culture demands of us. There are some real problems with projecting the perfect image. First of all, it's simply not true—we are not always happy, optimistic, in command. Second, projecting the flawless image keeps us from reaching people who feel we just wouldn't understand them. And third, even if we could live a life with no conflict, suffering, or mistakes, it would be a shallow existence. The Christian with depth is the person who has failed and who has learned to live with it.

Procrastination is perhaps the worst, the most damaging failure of all. We who believe in Jesus, who hope in vindication, who proclaim the love of the heavenly Father, waste our time trying to avoid the things that are most important. How much faith, how much hope, how much love does the perpetual procrastinator really have?[3]

As you go through life, if you acquire any self-awareness, any kind of honest insight into your own personality, you know pretty well what your weaknesses are. You know how you are going to evade the responsibility of faith, hope, and love that Jesus offers. If you're honest, you know that you can't scapegoat—that you can't say it was somebody else's fault. You know that when it comes time for rendering an account of your life, you will be blamed or praised not for what the Pope has done, not for what the bishop has done, not for what the pastor has done (unless you are the pastor). All of us will be blamed or praised according to whether we have accepted the invitation to believe the message.

In the final analysis, the real challenge of Christian growth is the challenge of personal responsibility. The Spirit of Jesus calls out a second time: Are you going to take charge of your life today? Are you going to be responsible for what you do? Are you going to believe?

Perhaps we are all in the position of the man in Morton Kelsey's story who came to the edge of an abyss. As he stood there wondering what to so next, he was amazed to discover a tightrope stretched across the abyss. And slowly, surely, across the rope came an acrobat pushing before him a wheelbarrow with another performer in it. When they finally reached the safety of solid ground, the acrobat smiled at the man's amazement. "Don't you think I can do it again?" he asked. And the man replied, "Why yes, I certainly believe you can." The acrobat put his question again, and when the answer was the same, he pointed to the wheelbarrow and said, "Good! Then get in and I will take you across."

What did the traveler do? This is just the question we have to ask ourselves about Jesus Christ. Do we state our belief in him in no uncertain terms, even in finely articulated creeds, and then refuse to get into the wheelbarrow? What we do about the lordship of Jesus is a better indication of our faith than what we think. This is what the world wants from our rhetoric, what the man of God longs for in shepherds—daring enough to be different, humble enough to make mistakes, wild enough to be burnt in the fire of love, real enough to make others see how phony we are.

Let the prayer of Nikos Kazantzakis arise from our hearts at a passionate pitch of loving awareness:

I am a bow on your hands, Lord.
Draw me, lest I rot.
Do not overdraw me, Lord, I shall break.
Overdraw me, Lord, and who cares if I break?

Chapter 10

The Victorious Limp

The joyous tumult from the Mount Zion Temple Fellowship thundered through the neighborhood. "Amen, brother! Preach it! Tell it like it is!" Rev. Moses Mowinkle was under the anointing. His melodious baritone soared to the heavens, mellowed into the bleating of a lamb, and finally faded to a whisper. As his sermon ended, two hundred worshipers erupted into praise, dancing, weeping, and unrestrained joy. The three- hour worship service ended at noon and the faith community filed into the street. They all lived on Lemmon Street, the black ghetto.

It was Baltimore in 1938.

Racism was deeply implanted in the city. Blacks were considered separate but unequal. They were tolerated as long as they knew their "place" and stayed in it. The superiority of the white man was universally acknowledged as was the inferiority of "niggers," as everyone in the neighborhood called them. If some uppity nigger lost his senses and ventured into an upscale haberdashery in the white part of town, he was not allowed to try on the garments before his possible purchase. After all, a white customer might arrive later and don the same jacket.

The blacks lived in dilapidated shanties: the windows on the second floor offered a splendid view of the white man's garbage cans. For the most part, the Mt. Zion Temple Fellowship stayed to themselves.

Meanwhile, the raging theological debate uptown was: how could God have allowed the nigger Joe Louis to become the heavyweight champion of the world? Was God exacting vengeance on white people for some unrepented sin? Was it simply the cruel hoax of a whimsical Deity? Or maybe as Woody Allen would put it years later: "It's not that God is cruel; it's just that God is an underachiever." Could it be there is no God?

Faith had been restored in 1936 when the great White Hope from Nazi Germany, Max Schmeling, battered Louis mercilessly for eleven rounds and then floored him with a KO punch in the twelfth. God's honor was vindicated and white supremacy restored.

A rematch between the Brown Bomber from Detroit and the White Hope from Munich was scheduled for the summer of 1938. Caucasian expectations in Baltimore soared. It was Armageddon, the powers of darkness against the power of light.

In his Pulitzer prize-winning autobiography, *Growing Up*, Russell Baker writes:

At last the night of the titanic battle finally arrived and I settled by my radio to attend upon the pivotal point of the modern age. . . .

At the bell Louis left his corner, appraised Schmeling the way a butcher eyes a side of beef, then punched him senseless in two minutes and nine seconds. Paralyzing in its brutal suddenness, it was the ultimate anticlimax for the white race.

From Lemmon Street I heard the customary whooping and cheering. I went to the kitchen window. . . . People were streaming out into the alley, pounding each other delightedly on the back and roaring with exultation. Then I saw someone start to move up the alley, out toward white territory, and the rest of the group, seized by an instinct to defy destiny, falling in behind him and moving en masse. . . .

There they were, marching right out into the middle of Lombard Street as though it was their own street. . . .

Joe Louis had given them the courage to assert their right to use a public thoroughfare, and there wasn't a white person down there to dispute it. It was the first civil rights demonstration I ever saw and it was completely spontaneous, ignited by the finality with which Joe Louis had destroyed the theory of white supremacy. The march lasted maybe five minutes, only as long as it took the entire throng to move slowly down the full length of the block. Then they turned the corner and went back into the alleys and, I guess, felt better than most of them had felt for a long time.[1]

Does this sound like the victorious life in Christ? No! It was one of the many faces'of the victorious limp.

Fifty years after Louis's first-round knockout, there are parts of America where to be black is not to be beautiful but bastard. Tonight one person in five in the United States will go to bed hungry. Thirty million more are undernourished. Many are committed Christians. Is this the victorious life?

When our social system condemned blacks to the back of the bus, forced them to study in shacks and work in toilets, forbade them our sidewalks and our pews, barred them from hotels and restaurants, from movie theaters and restrooms, was this the victorious life?

Most of the descriptions of the victorious life do not match the reality of my own. Hyperbole, bloated rhetoric, and grandiose testimonies create the impression that once Jesus is acknowledged as Lord, the Christian life becomes a picnic on a green lawn—marriage blossoms into connubial bliss, physical health flourishes, acne disappears, and sinking careers suddenly soar. The victorious life is proclaimed to mean that everybody is a winner. An attractive twenty-year-old accepts Jesus and becomes Miss America, a floundering lawyer conquers alcoholism and whips F. Lee Bailey in court, a tenth-round draft choice for the Green Bay Packers goes to the Pro Bowl. Miracles occur, conversions abound, church attendance skyrockets, ruptured relationships get healed, shy people become gregarious, and the Atlanta Braves win the World Series. Idyllic descriptions of victory in Jesus are more often colored by cultural and personal expectations than by Christ and the ragamuffin gospel.

The New Testament depicts another picture of the victorious life . . . Jesus on Calvary. The biblical image of the victorious life reads more like the victorious limp. Jesus was victorious not because he never flinched, talked back, or questioned, but having flinched, talked back, and questioned, *he remained faithful.*

What makes authentic disciples is not visions, ecstasies, biblical mastery of chapter and verse, or spectacular success in the ministry, but a capacity for faithfulness. Buffeted by the fickle winds of failure, battered by their own unruly emotions, and bruised by rejection and ridicule, authentic disciples may have stumbled and frequently fallen, endured lapses and relapses, gotten handcuffed to the fleshpots and wandered into a far country. Yet, they kept coming back to Jesus.

After life has lined their faces a little, many followers of Jesus come into a coherent sense of themselves for the first time. When they modestly claim, "I am still a ragamuffin, but I'm different" they are right. Where sin abounded, grace has more abounded.

The portrait of Peter, the rock who proved to be a sand pile, speaks to every ragamuffin across the generations. Lloyd Ogilvie notes: "Peter had built his whole relationship with Jesus Christ on his assumed capacity to be adequate. That's why he took his denial of the Lord so hard. His strength, loyalty, and faithfulness were his self-generated assets of discipleship. The fallacy in Peter's mind was this: he believed his relationship was dependent on his consistency in producing the qualities he thought had earned him the Lord's approval.

"Many of us face the same problem. We project into the Lord our own measured standard of acceptance. Our whole understanding of him is based in a *quid pro quo* of bartered love. He will love us if we are good, moral, and diligent. But we have turned the tables; we try to live so that he will love us, rather than living because he has already loved us."[2]

During the supper of his love, Jesus turned and said to Peter: "I tell you solemnly, this very night, before the cock crows, you will have disowned me three times." Remember Peter's hollow boast? "Even if I have to die with you, I will never disown you." Brimming with confidence, Peter relied on his own resources. But today these words are a song of praise to Peter. His restoration to grace proved to be such a recreation that his protest is no longer an empty boast but a prophecy of God's unyielding truth. For Peter will die rather than betray his Master, and he will forever remember his unfaithfulness as the moment of the triumph of grace and Christ's conquering love.

A story: Virtuoso violinist Pinchas Zukerman was giving a master class to a group of young artists who had come to the Aspen Music Festival from the four corners of the world. The auditorium was filled with their peers and distinguished teachers and performers; the atmosphere was electric. To each of the talented performers Zukerman offered friendly advice and encouragement, discussing their playing in detail, and invariably picking up his own violin to demonstrate finer points of technique and interpretation.

Finally came the turn of a young musician who performed brilliantly. When the applause subsided, Zukerman complimented the artist, then walked over to his own violin, caressed it, tucked it under his chin, paused a long moment, and then, without playing a note or uttering a word, gently placed it back in its case. Once more, the applause broke out, and this time it was deafening, in recognition of the master, who could pay so gracious a compliment.[3]

After his triple denial, what future would have awaited Peter if he had had to depend on my patience, understanding, and compassion? Instead of a shrug, sneer, slap, or curse, Jesus responded with the subtlest and most gracious compliment imaginable. He named Peter the leader of the faith community and entrusted him with authority to preach the Good News in the power of the Spirit.

The limping Peter's betrayal of the Master, like so many of our own moral relapses and refusals of grace, was not a terminal failure but the occasion for painful personal growth in fidelity. It is not unrealistic to presume that later, Peter praised God for the servant girl in Caiaphas's courtyard who turned him into a sniveling coward. In this context, small wonder that Augustine would paraphrase the words of Paul, "That for those who love God everything works unto good, even sin."

At some point in each of our lives, we were deeply touched by a profound encounter with Jesus Christ. It was a mountaintop experience, a moment of immense consolation. We were swept up in peace, joy, certitude, love. Quite simply, we were overcome. Our minds and hearts resonated with awe and wonder. We were deeply moved for a few hours, days, or weeks, and eventually returned to the routine occupations of our daily existence. We did not get unraveled.

Slowly we got caught up in the demands of ministry or career and the distractions our busy world offers. We began to treat Jesus like the old friend from Brooklyn whom we dearly loved in years past but have gradually lost track of. Of course, it was unintentional. We simply allowed circumstances to drive us apart. On a recent visit to that city it never crossed our mind to contact him. We had become preoccupied with something else, even though it was far less lifegiving and captivating. It is possible we may never love anyone as much as we loved him, but even the memory has grown dim.

Heightened by the agnosticism of inattention—the lack of personal discipline over media bombardment, mind control, sterile conversation, private prayer, and the subjugation of the senses—the presence of Jesus grows more and more remote. Just as the failure to be attentive dissolves confidence and communion in a human relationship, so inattention to the Holy unravels the fabric of the divine relationship. "Thorns and thistles choke the unused path." A verdant heart becomes a devastated vineyard. As we periodically close off God to our consciousness by looking the other way, our hearts are chilled. Christian agnostics don't deny a personal God; they display their unbelief by ignoring the sacred. The paltriness of our lives is mute testimony to the shabby furniture of our souls.

And so our days become more and more trivial. "We get caught in a hectic maze. Rising when the clock determines. Battered by news headlines that seem remote and beyond our reach. Jangled by all the mechanical operations that launch us into activity and productivity. Tested by traffic, forced to calculate time and distance to the second. Elevators and phones and gadgets guide us through necessary interactions and keep human interactions superficial and at a minimum. Our concentration is interspersed by meetings and small crises. At the end of the day we rewind ourselves: traffic, automation, headlines, until we set that alarm clock to dictate tomorrow's awakening. Routines of ticking and timing. Little room for responding humanly and humanely to the day's events; little time to enter into the wisdom and freshness and the promise of its opportunities. We feel our lives closing in, confining, and conforming us."[4]

We settle in and settle down to lives of comfortable piety and well-fed virtue. We grow complacent and lead practical lives. Our feeble attempts at prayer are filled with stilted phrases addressed to an impassive deity. Even times of worship become trivialized.

This is the victorious limp often lived by this writer. At different times on the journey I have tried to fill the emptiness that frequently comes with God's presence through a variety of substitutes—writing, preaching, traveling, television, movies, ice cream, shallow relationships, sports, music, daydreaming, alcohol, etc. As Annie Dillard says, "There is always an enormous temptation to diddle around making itsy-bitsy friends and meals and journeys for itsy-bitsy years on end."[5] Along the way I opted for slavery and lost the desire for freedom. I loved my captivity and I imprisoned myself in the desire for things I hated. I hardened my heart against true love. I abandoned prayer and took flight from the simple sacredness of my life. On some given day when grace overtook me and I returned to prayer, I half-expected Jesus to ask, "Who dat?"

None of my failures in faithfulness have proved terminal. Again and again radical grace has gripped me in the depths of my being, brought me to accept ownership of my infidelities, and led me back to the fifth step of the AA program: "Acknowledge to God, another human being, and myself the exact nature of my wrongdoing."

The forgiveness of God is gratuitous liberation from guilt. Paradoxically, the conviction of personal sinfulness becomes the occasion of encounter with the merciful love of the redeeming God. "There is more joy in heaven over one sinner who repents . . ." (Luke 15:7). In his brokenness, the repentant prodigal knew an intimacy with his father that his sinless, self-righteous brother would never know.

When Jesus forgave the sins of the paralytic, some scribes thought to themselves: "God alone can forgive sins" (Mark 2:7). How enlightened they were in their blindness! Only God knows how to pardon. Our clumsy human attempts at forgiveness often create more problems than they solve. In condescending fashion we crush and humiliate the sinner with our unbearable largesse. He may feel forgiven but utterly bereft of reassurance, consolation, and encouragement. Only God knows how to pardon and put all four together. The prodigal's father said in effect: "Hush, child. I don't need to know where you've been or what you've been up to."

The gospel of grace announces: forgiveness precedes repentance. The sinner is accepted before he pleads for mercy. It is already granted. He need only receive it. Total amnesty. Gratuitous pardon. "God alone can make forgiveness something glorious to remember. He's so glad to absolve us that those who've afforded him that joy feel, not like disagreeable, troublesome pests, but like pampered children, understood and heartened, pleasing and useful to him, and infinitely better than they thought. 'O happy fault!' they could cry. If we weren't sinners and didn't need pardon more than bread, we'd have no way of knowing how deep God's love is."[6]

When the prodigal son limped home from his lengthy binge of waste and wandering, boozing and womanizing, his motives were mixed at best. He said to himself, "How many of my father's paid servants have more food than they want, and here am I dying of hunger! I will leave this place and go to my father" (Luke 15:17-18). The ragamuffin stomach was not churning with compunction because he had broken his father's heart. He stumbled home simply to survive. His sojourn in a far country had left him bankrupt. The days of wine and roses had left him dazed and disillusioned. The wine soured and the roses withered. His declaration of independence had reaped an unexpected harvest: not freedom, joy, and new life but bondage, gloom, and a brush with death. His fair-weather friends had shifted their allegiance when his piggy bank emptied. Disenchanted with life, the wastrel weaved his way home, not from a burning desire to see his father, but just to stay alive.

For me, the most touching verse in the entire Bible is the father's response: "While he was still a long way off, his father saw him and was moved with pity. He ran to the boy, clasped him in his arms and kissed him tenderly" (Luke 15:20). I am moved that the father didn't cross-examine the boy, bully him, lecture him on ingratitude, or insist on any high motivation. He was so overjoyed at the sight of his son that he ignored all the canons of prudence and parental discretion and simply welcomed him home. The father took him back just as he was.

What a word of encouragement, consolation and comfort! We don't have to sift our heart's and analyze our intentions before returning home. Abba just wants us to show up. We don't have to tarry at the tavern until purity of heart arrives. We don't have to be shredded with sorrow or crushed with contrition. We don't have to be perfect or even very good before God will accept us. We don't have to wallow in guilt, shame, remorse, and self- condemnation. Even if we still nurse a secret nostalgia for the far country, Abba falls on our neck and kisses us.

Even if we come back because we couldn't make it on our own, God will welcome us. He will seek no explanations about our sudden appearance. He is glad we are there and wants to give us all we desire.

Henri Nouwen writes: "In my mind's eye, I see Rembrandt's painting *The Return of the Prodigal Son.* The dim-eyed old father holds his returned son close to his chest with an unconditional love. Both of his hands, one strong and masculine, the other gentle and feminine, rest on his son's shoulders. He does not look at his son but feels his young, tired body and lets him rest in his embrace. His immense red cape is like the wings of a mother bird covering her fragile nestling. He seems to think only one thing: he is back home, and I am so glad to have him with me again.

"So why delay? God is standing there with open arms, waiting to embrace me. He won't ask any questions about my past. Just having me back is all he desires."[7]

The parable of the prodigal is one of the many faces of faithfulness. It is also an earthy and honest portrait of the victorious limp.

So is the Academy Award winning film of 1966, *A Man For All Seasons,* the gripping narrative of one man's faithfulness to himself and to Christ at all costs. Thomas More, the Chancellor of England, has been imprisoned in the Tower of London for his refusal to obey the Crown. He is visited by his daughter Meg who pleads with him to change his mind and save his life. More explains that if he took the oath of allegiance to King Henry VIII, he would compromise his conscience and betray Jesus.

She argues that it is not his fault that the state is three-quarters bad and, if he chooses to suffer for it, he is making himself a hero. Her father replies: "Meg, if we lived in a state where virtue was profitable, common sense would make us good, and greed would make us saintly. And we'd live animals or angels in the happy land that needs no heroes. But since in fact we see that avarice, anger, envy, pride, sloth, lust, and stupidity commonly profit far beyond humility, chastity, fortitude, justice and thought, and have to choose to be human at all, why then perhaps we must stand fast a little, even at the risk of being heroes."[8]

In 1535 More went to the scaffold cheerfully in the royal freedom of a Christian man. He prayed briefly for God's mercy, embraced the executioner—who begged his forgiveness—confessed his Christian faith, and called on all present to pray for the King, saying that he died "the King's good servant, but God's first." His last words were a joke about his beard, which he arranged on the block so that it should not be cut, since his beard at least had committed no treason.

Thomas More, a man of the world in secular dress living in a secular city and surrounded by family, possessions, and the duties of public life, was *faithful.* Not because he was without faults and sins; he had them, like every one of us, and confessed them often before his death. But with all his weaknesses and flaws he made a radical choice to be true to himself and his Christ in the supreme test of martyrdom.

In 1929 G.K. Chesterton predicted: "Sir Thomas More is more important at this moment than at any moment since his death, even perhaps the great moment of dying; but he is not quite so important as he will be in a hundred years time."[9] His life is a timeless statement—it is possible to live in this world soberly, honestly, unfanatically, unpietistically, seriously and at the same time joyfully: faithful. What is the message of this man's life? Make a radical choice in faith, despite all your sinfulness, and sustain it through ordinary daily life for Christ the Lord and his kingdom.

The mature Christians I have met along the way are those who have failed and have learned to live gracefully with their failure. Faithfulness requires the courage to risk everything on Jesus, the willingness to keep growing, and the readiness to risk failure throughout our lives. What do these things mean, specifically?

Risking everything on Jesus: the ragamuffin gospel says we can't lose, because we have nothing to lose. Faithfulness to Jesus implies that with all our sins, scars, and insecurities, we stand with him; that we are formed and informed by his Word; that we acknowledge that abortion and nuclear weapons are two sides of the same hot coin minted in hell; that we stand upright beside the Prince of Peace and refuse to bow before the shrine of national security; that we are a life-giving and not a death-dealing people of God; that we live under the sign of the cross and not the sign of the bomb.

The willingness to keep growing: Unfaithfulness is a refusal to become, a rejection of grace (grace that is inactive is an illusion), and the refusal to be oneself. Long ago I read a prayer composed by the late General Douglas MacArthur: "Youth is not a period of time. It is a state of mind, a result of the will, a quality of the imagination, a victory of courage over timidity, of the taste for adventure over the love of comfort. A man doesn't grow old because he has lived a certain number of years. A man grows old when he deserts his ideal. The years may wrinkle his skin, but deserting his ideal wrinkles his soul. Preoccupations, fears, doubts, and despair are the enemies which slowly bow us toward earth and turn us into dust before death. You will remain young as long as you are open to what is beautiful, good and great; receptive to the messages of other men and women, of nature and of God. If one day you should become bitter, pessimistic, and gnawed by despair, may God have mercy on your old man's soul."

The readiness to risk failure: Many of us are haunted by our failure to have done with our lives what we longed to accomplish. The disparity between our ideal self and our real self, the grim specter of past infidelities, the awareness that I am not living what I believe, the relentless pressure of conformity, and the nostalgia for lost innocence reinforces a nagging sense of existential guilt: I have failed. This is the cross we never expected, and the one we find hardest to bear.

One morning at prayer, I heard this word: "Little brother, I witnessed a Peter who claimed that he did not know me, a James who wanted power in return for service to the kingdom, a Philip who failed to see the Father in me, and scores of disciples who were convinced I was finished on Calvary. The New Testament has many examples of men and women who started out well and then faltered along the way.

"Yet on Easter night I appeared to Peter. James is not remembered for his ambition but for the sacrifice of his life for me. Philip did see the Father in me when I pointed the way, and the disciples who despaired had enough courage to recognize me when we broke bread at the end of the road to Emmaus. My point, little brother, is this: *I expect more failure from you than you expect from yourself.*"

The ragamuffin who sees his life as a voyage of discovery and runs the risk of failure has a better feel for faithfulness than the timid man who hides behind the law and never finds out who he is at all. Winston Churchill said it well: "Success is never final; failure is never fatal. It is courage that counts."

One night a dear friend of Roslyn's named Joe McGill was praying over this passage in John: "In the beginning was the Word, and the Word was with God and the Word was God. . . . The Word was made flesh, he lived among us. . . ." (John 1:1, 14). In the bright darkness of faith, he heard Jesus say: "Yes, the Word was made flesh. I chose to enter your broken world and limp through life with you."

On the last day, when we arrive at the Great Cabin in the Sky, many of us will be bloodied, battered, bruised, and limping. But, by God and by Christ, there will be a light in the window and a "welcome home" sign on the door.

Chapter 11

A Touch of Folly

In 1982 when I moved from Clearwater, Florida to New Orleans, and Roslyn and I began our life together, I did some homework on the origins of the Christian faith in the area. In sifting through the archives, I came across a fascinating piece of information.

Over a hundred years ago in the Deep South, a phrase so common in our Christian culture today, *born again*, was seldom or never used. Rather, the phrase used to describe the breakthrough into a personal relationship with Jesus Christ was, "I was seized by the power of a great affection."

These words describe both the initiative of God and the explosion within the heart when Jesus, instead of being a face on a holy card with long hair and a robe with many folds, becomes real, alive, and Lord of one's personal and professional life. Seized by the power of a great affection was a visceral description of the phenomenon of Pentecost, authentic conversion, and the release of the Holy Spirit. The phrase lent new meaning to the old Russian proverb, "Those who have the disease called Jesus will never be cured."

In March 1986 I was privileged to spend an afternoon with an Amish family in Lancaster, Pennsylvania. I have long cherished a deep respect and admiration for the Amish community. We each have a dream, a vision of life, that corresponds to our convictions, embodies our uniqueness, and expresses what is life-giving within us. Whether altruistic or ignoble, the dream gives definition to our lives, influences the decisions we make, the steps we take, and the words we speak. Daily we make choices that are either consistent with or contrary to our vision. A life of integrity is born of fidelity to the dream. As a community, the Amish, at great personal cost, have carved out a lifestyle that gives flesh and bone to their dream.

Jonas Zook is an eighty-two-year-old widower. He and his children raise piglets for their livelihood. The oldest, Barbara, fifty-seven, manages the household. The three younger children, Rachel, fifty-three, Elam, forty-seven, and Sam, forty-five, are all severely retarded. When I arrived at noon with two friends, little Elam—about four feet tall, heavy-set, thickly bearded, and wearing the black Amish outfit with the circular hat—was coming out of the barn some fifty yards away, pitchfork in hand. He had never laid eyes on me in his life; yet, when he saw me step out of the car, this little Mongoloid dropped the pitchfork and ran lickety-split in my direction. Two feet away, he flung himself at me, wrapped his arms around my neck, his legs around my waist, and kissed me on the lips with fierce intensity for a full thirty seconds.

Well, I was temporarily stunned and terribly self-conscious. But in the twinkle of an eye, Jesus set me free from propriety. I buried my lips into Elam's and returned his kiss with the same enthusiasm. Then he jumped down, wrapped both his hands around my right arm, and led me on a tour of the farm.

A half hour later, Elam sat next to me at lunch. Midway through the meal I turned around to say something. Inadvertently, my right elbow slammed into Elam's rib cage. He didn't wince, he didn't groan. He wept like a two-year-old child. His next move undid me.

Elam came over to my chair, planted himself on my lap, and kissed me even harder on the lips. Then he kissed my eyes, nose, forehead, and cheeks.

And there was Brennan, dazed, dumbstruck, weeping, and suddenly *seized by the power of a great affection.* In his utter simplicity little Elam Zook was an icon of Jesus Christ. Why? Because at that moment his love for me did not stem from any attractiveness or lovability of mine. It was not conditioned by any response on my part. Elam loved me whether I was kind or unkind, pleasant or nasty. His love arose from a source outside of himself and myself.

As often happens in a profound moment like that, I will recall a line from a book I had read years earlier. Discussing the tragic history of native Americans, the author noted that the Iroquois Indians attributed divinity to retarded children, gave them an honored place in the tribe, and treated them as gods. In their unselfconscious freedom they were a transparent window into the Great Spirit—into the heart of Jesus Christ who loves us as we are and not as we should be, in the state of grace or disgrace, beyond caution, boundary, regret, or breaking point.[1]

In a world that is torn and tearing, it takes a touch of folly to believe that "even when our choices are destructive and their consequences hurtful, God's love remains unwavering. Thus, regardless of our own insulation and defensiveness, God is constantly open and vulnerable to us."[2] As the sea of suffering humanity swells, we are hard pressed for proofs that the crucified risen Jesus has prevailed over every principality, power, and dominion, discarded them like a garment, and led them captive in his victory procession.

The sad plight of Native Americans is a haunting memory that refuses to go away. They are homeless, having lost their culture, their land, their pride, and their hope.

Refugees from Afghanistan, Haiti, Cuba, and the South Pacific Islands stream to our shores and are often deposited in slums and barrios unfit for human habitation. Bag ladies, derelicts, and the mentally disturbed stalk the street of our cities. Small farmers are wiped out by the encroachment of agribusiness. Strip-mining has raped the land. White collar crime on Wall Street and governmental fraud in Washington devastate American morale. AIDS victims are ostracized and shunned as undesirables. The drug epidemic ravages our youth and puts all our tomorrows up for grabs. Venal clergymen are a dime a dozen. Anti-Semitism and racism are scars on the national conscience. After two thousand years the Body of Christ is still dreadfully divided by doctrine, history, and day-to-day living.

Scabrous stories about Christian disunity pepper the pages of periodicals and newspapers. The Body of Truth is bleeding from a thousand wounds.

Small wonder that many Christians today are bedraggled, beat-up, and burnt-out. The bleak landscape of the global village has introduced discouragement, disillusionment, and what Parker Palmer calls "functional atheism"—the belief that nothing is happening unless we are making it happen. Though our Christian language pays lip-service to God, our way of functioning assumes that God is dead or in a coma. Being seized by the power of a great affection does not seem to relate to the real world in which we live. Does it not require a fair measure of lunacy to listen to the looney tunes of the ragamuffin gospel?

Yes it does! As Zorba the Greek said to his employer: "It's difficult, boss, very difficult. You need a touch of folly to do it; folly, do you see? You have to risk everything." In the final analysis, discipleship is a life of sublime madness.

The truth of the Gospel of Jesus Christ does not rise and fall on the issues of corrupt clergy, the exploitation of the poor, the stinginess of multinationals or the irrational fanaticism of modern dictatorships. It deserves to be accepted or rejected for what it is: an answer to the most fundamental questions a person may ask—is life absurd or does it have a purpose? Jesus replies that not only do our lives have purpose but God has directly intervened in human affairs to make abundantly clear what that purpose is.

What is the nature of Ultimate Reality? Jesus responds that the Really Real is generous, forgiving, saving love.

In the end, will life triumph over death? With unshaken confidence Jesus answers: the kingdom of my Father cannot be overcome, even by death. In the end everything will be all right, nothing can harm you permanently; no loss is lasting, no defeat more than transitory, no disappointment is conclusive. Suffering, failure, loneliness, sorrow, discouragement, and death will be part of your journey, but the kingdom of God will conquer all these horrors. No evil can resist grace forever.

If you reject the ragamuffin gospel and turn your back on Christianity, do so because you find the answers of Jesus incredible, blasphemous, or hopelessly hopeful. "Reject Christianity if you will out of motives of cynicism, turn away from it because you believe Reality is malign and punitive; choose a God that is cantankerous, vindictive, or forgetful, or determined to keep man in his place, if such a God is more to your choosing. If you cannot accept the idea that love is at the core of the universe, that is your privilege. If you do not believe that the Absolute passionately wants to be our friend and our lover, then by all means reject such a seemingly absurd notion. If you do not believe that we have the enthusiasm, and the strength, and the courage, and the creativity to love one another as friends, then quickly cast aside such an incredible idea into the trash can. And if you think it is ridiculous to believe that life will triumph over death, then don't bother with Christianity, because you can't be a Christian unless you believe that."[3]

In first-century Palestine, the people of Judea and Galilee fudged and hedged on the proclamation of the Reign of God. Jesus announced that the old era was done, that a new age had dawned, and the only appropriate response was to be captivated with joy and wonder.

His listeners did not say, "Yes, rabbi, we believe you," or "No, rabbi, we think you are a fool." Rather, they said, "What about the sap-suckin' Romans?" or "When are you going to produce an apocalyptic sign?" or "Why aren't you and your disciples within the Jewish Law?" or "Whose side do you take in the various legal controversies?"

Jesus replied that the Romans were not the issue, the Law was not the issue, and cosmic miracles were not the issue. The relentless love of God was the issue, and in the face of that revelation, the Romans and the Torah were secondary. But his audience stubbornly refused to concede that the Torah could possibly be secondary or that the Roman domination of Palestine could be marginal. The Torah and Rome—these were the relevant issues, the gut problems. "What do you have to say about them, rabbi?"

Once again Jesus responded that he did not come to discuss the Law nor to challenge the Roman Empire. He had come to herald the Good News that the Really Real is love and to invite men and women to a joyous response to that love.

Sober, hard-headed, realistic critics simply shook their heads. "Why doesn't he address the critical questions?"

Since the day that Jesus first appeared on the scene, we have developed vast theological systems, organized world-wide churches, filled libraries with brilliant Christological scholarship, engaged in earth-shaking controversies and embarked on crusades, reforms, and renewals. Yet there are still precious few of us with sufficient folly to make the mad exchange of everything for Christ; only a remnant with the confidence to risk everything on the gospel of grace; only a minority who stagger about with the delirious joy of the man who found the buried treasure.

It was cynicism, pessimism, and despair that shadowed the ministry of Jesus and, as the old French proverb goes, *"Plus ça change, plus c'est la meme chose"*—the more things change, the more they stay the same.

At the risk of sounding like a country cracker cowboy preacher, allow me to raise some intimate, personal questions about your relationship with Jesus of Nazareth. Do you live each day in the blessed assurance that you have been saved by the unique grace of our Lord Jesus Christ? After falling flat on your face, are you still firmly convinced that the fundamental structure of reality is not works but grace? Are you moody and melancholy because you are still striving for the perfection that comes from your own efforts and not from faith in Jesus Christ? Are you shocked and horrified when you fail? Are you really aware that you don't have to change, grow, or be good to be loved?

Are you as certain of the triumph of good over evil as the fermentation of dough by yeast? Though on a given day you may be more depressed than anything else, is the general orientation of your life toward peace and joy? Are you diminished by other people's perception of you or your own definition of yourself? Do you possess that touch of folly to transcend doubt, fear, and self-hatred and accept that you are accepted?

If not, you probably belong to the brotherhood of the bedraggled, beat-up, and burnt-out. You may feel like a charred log in a fireplace, totally drained of energy, and unable to light a fire in yourself. Your personal inner resources appear to be exhausted.

Louis Savary describes the brotherhood this way: "Their life is full of demands from others. They seem to be living at least three lives; everyone wants a piece of them; they can't say no yet they have no time to do what they have already said yes to. . . . They cannot seem to find the necessary clarity and information on which to base decisions . . . they make a great investment in relationships and get little gratitude, feedback, or even acknowledgment from others. 'Although nonreciprocity is inevitable and acceptable,' writes Mitchell, 'it is also draining. No one can function long in a helping profession without feeling its impact.' "[4]

The first step toward rejuvenation begins with accepting where you are and exposing your poverty, frailty, and emptiness to the love that is everything. Don't try to feel anything, think anything, or do anything. With all the goodwill in the world you cannot make anything happen. Don't force prayer. Simply relax in the presence of the God you half believe in and ask for a touch of folly.

The Indian poet Tagore puts it this way:

No, it is not yours to open buds into blossom.
Shake the bud, strike it,
it is beyond your power to make it blossom.
Your touch soils it.
You tear its petals to pieces
and strew them in the dust,
But no colors appear and no perfume.
Oh, it is not for you to open the bud into
blossom.

He who can open the bud does it so simply.
He gives it a glance and the life sap stirs
    through its veins.
At his breath the flower spreads its wings
and flutters in the wind.
Colors flash out like heart longing,
the perfume betrays a sweet secret.
He who can open the bud does it so simply.

Next, try this simple exercise in faith: gently close your eyes and assume any position that is comfortable so long as you keep your spine straight—standing, sitting, kneeling or lying on your back with your knees bent. Imagine Jesus glancing at you either the way he glanced at the apostle John in the Upper Room when, in an incredible gesture of intimacy he, laid his head on Jesus' chest, or the way he looked at the sinful woman washing his feet with her tears and drying them with her hair. For ten minutes pray over and over the first strophe of Psalm 23: "The Lord is my shepherd, I lack nothing" (JB).

For the next ten minutes pray over this passage from Hosea and wherever you see the word *Israel*, replace it with your own name:

Israel, how could I give you up?
My heart turns against it.
When Israel was a child I loved him,
I myself taught him to walk,
I took him in my arms;
Yet he has not understood that I was the one
    looking after him.
I led him with reins of kindness,
with leading-strings of love.
I was like someone who lifts an infant close
    against his cheek;

stooping down to him I gave him his food.
How could I treat you like Admah,
or deal with you like Zeboiim?
My heart recoils from it,
my whole being trembles at the thought.
I will not give reign to my fierce anger,
I will not destroy Ephraim again,
for I am God, not man:
I am the holy one in your midst
and have no wish to destroy" (Hosea 11:1a, 3-4,
    8c-9, NAB).

Finally, for the last five minutes of this faith exercise read aloud slowly these three texts:

This is why I am going to lure her and lead her into the wilderness and speak to her heart. I am going to give her back her vineyards, and make the Valley of Achor a gateway of hope. Then she will respond to me as she did when she was young, and she did when she came out of the land of Egypt (Hosea 2:14-15).

The Lord called me from the womb, from the body of my mother he named my name . . . Does a woman forget her baby at the breast, or fail to cherish the son of her womb? Yet even if these I forget, I will never forget you. See I have branded you on the palms of my hands, your ramparts are always under my eye (Isaiah 49:1, 15-16).

In face of all this, what is there left to say? If God is for us, who can be against us? He who did not hesitate to give what was most precious to himself—gave as a matter of fact over into our hands—can we not trust such a God to give us, with him, everything else that we need? (Romans 8:31-32).

Should you ever have the opportunity to celebrate Easter in France, whether it be a large metropolis such as Paris, Bordeaux, Lyon, or Dijon or a small village such as Saint-Remy (where I lived for six months), you will see one phrase written on the walls of buildings or the sides of buses in script or black print. You will hear the one phrase sung, chanted, and recited in the churches; you will hear it exchanged as an Easter greeting as people pass on the street: *"L'amour de Dieu est folie!"*—The love of God is folly.

In these pages I have stuttered and stammered in a halting attempt to hint at the shattering reality of the furious love of God. Like an old miner panning the stream of his memories, I have reached back into the Scriptures to listen to God's self-disclosure. I have read hundreds of biblical, theological, and spiritual books seeking deeper understanding of the gospel of grace. I have freely employed story, imagery, poetry, symbolism, the language of metaphor and prose narrative to communicate something of the passionate love of our passionate God. Acknowledging my own limitations, I am not going to be hard on myself because I know there is going to come a time and there is going to be a place where we can say it all. The secret of the mystery is: God is always greater. No matter how great we think him to be, his love is always greater.

The story goes that Thomas Aquinas, perhaps the world's greatest theologian, toward the end of his life suddenly stopped writing. When his secretary complained that his work was unfinished, Thomas replied: "Brother Reginald, when I was at prayer a few months ago, I experienced something of the reality of Jesus Christ. That day, I lost all appetite for writing. In fact, all I have ever written about Christ seems now to me to be like straw."[5]

L'amour de Dieu est folie! It reaches out to raga-muffins everywhere. My only exhortation—let us walk together. My only prayer—may Jesus Christ convert us to the folly of the gospel.

A Word After

Upon finishing *The Ragamuffin Gospel,* a thoughtful reader might ruminate, "Hmmm. He made a few good points, but the book seems one-sided. Brennan goes on and on about Abba, Jesus, radical grace, compassion, and the furious love of God, but says little about morality. I think he stacked the deck."

The Bible is the love story of God with his people. God calls, pursues, forgives, and heals. Our response to his love is itself his gift.

Let us suppose you advanced me $1 million for my personal needs. A year later, you request that I begin making monthly interest-free payments of $10,000 on the debt. On the first day of each month I sit down to write the check just as the morning mail arrives. You have sent me a $10,000 check to cover my payment. You continue this practice until the full amount of my debt is relieved. I am bewildered and protest, "But this is totally lopsided."

God is enamored with his people and so intent upon a response that he even provides the grace to respond "May he enlighten your innermost vision that you may know the great hope to which he has called you, the wealth of his glorious heritage to be distributed among the members of the church, and the immeasurable scope of his power in us who believe" (Ephesians 1:18-19).

The love of God is simply unimaginable. "May Christ dwell in your hearts through faith, and may love be the root and foundation of your life. Thus you will be able to grasp fully, with all the holy ones, the breadth and length and height and depth of Christ's love, and experience this love *which surpasses all knowledge*, so that you may attain to the fullness of God himself" (Ephesians 3:17-19).

Do we really hear what Paul is saying? Stretch, man, stretch! Let go of impoverished, circumscribed, and finite perceptions of God. The love of Christ is beyond all knowledge, beyond anything we can intellectualize or imagine. It is not a mild benevolence but a consuming fire. Jesus is so unbearably forgiving, so infinitely patient and so unendingly loving that he provides us with the resources we need to live lives of gracious response. "Glory be to him whose power, working in us, can do infinitely more than we can ask or imagine" (Ephesians 3:20).

Does it sound like an easy religion?

Love has its own exigencies. It weighs and counts

nothing but expects everything. Perhaps that explains our reluctance to risk. We know only too well that the gospel of grace is an irresistible call to love the same way. No wonder so many of us elect to surrender our souls to rules rather than to living in union with Love.

No greater sinners exist than those so-called Christians who disfigure the face of God, mutilate the gospel of grace, and intimidate others through fear. They corrupt the essential nature of Christianity. In Eugene Peterson's forceful phrase, "They are telling lies about God, and let them be cursed."

The North American Church is at a critical juncture. The gospel of grace is being confused and compromised by silence, seduction, and outright subversion. The vitality of faith is jeopardized. The lying slogans of the fixers who carry religion like a sword of judgment pile up with impunity.

Let ragamuffins everywhere gather as a confessing Church to cry out in protest. Revoke the licenses of religious leaders who falsify the idea of God. Sentence them to three years in solitude with the Bible as their only companion.

Mary Magdalene stands as a witness par excellence to the ragamuffin gospel. On Good Friday she watched as the man she loved got blown away in the most brutal and dehumanizing fashion. The focus of her attention however was not on suffering but the suffering Christ "who loved me and delivered himself up for me" (Galatians 2:20). Never allow these words to be interpreted as allegory in the life of Magdalene. The love of Jesus was a burning and divine reality to her: she would have been buried in history as some unknown hooker save for the Christ encounter.

She has no understanding of God, church, religion, prayer or ministry except in terms of the Sacred Man who loved her and delivered himself up for her. The unique place that Magdalene occupies in the history of discipleship owes not to her mysterious love for Jesus but to the miraculous transformation that his love wrought in her life. She simply let herself be loved. "The central truth for which Mary's life has come to stand is that it is possible to be delivered through love from the lowest depths to the shining heights where God dwelleth."[1]

Where sin abounded, grace abounded all the more.

When Jesus asked Peter on the Tiberian seashore, "Simon, son of John, do you love me?" He added nothing else: what he said was enough. Do you love me? Can you allow my love to touch you in your weakness, set you free, and empower you there? Thereafter, the only power Peter had was Jesus' love for him. He told and retold the story of his own unfaithfulness and how Jesus touched him. When he proclaimed the gospel of grace, he preached from his weakness the power of God. That is what converted the Roman world and what will convert us, and the people around us, if they see the love of Christ has touched us.

The confessing church of American ragamuffins needs to join Magdalene and Peter in witnessing that Christianity is not primarily a moral code but a grace-laden mystery; it is not essentially a philosophy of love but a love affair; it is not keeping rules with clenched fists but receiving a gift with open hands.

Several years ago, the renowned evangelical theologian Francis Schaeffer wrote: True spirituality consists in living moment to moment by the grace of Jesus Christ. This book lays no claim to originality; it is simply a commentary on Schaeffer's statement. As C.S. Lewis was fond of saying: People need more to be reminded than to be instructed.

Notes

Chapter 1

1. Anthony De Mello, *Taking Flight: A Book of Story Meditations* (New York: Doubleday, 1988), p. 105.

2. Fyodor Dostoevsky, *Crime and Punishment*, trans. Constance Garnett (New York: Random House Inc., 1950), p. 322.

3. Jaroslav Pelikan, *Jesus Through the Centuries, His Place in History of Culture* (New Haven, Conn.: Yale University Press, 1985), p. 158. This is a work of vast and carefully concealed scholarship which traces the images of Jesus from New Testament times down to the twentieth century. Pelikan suggests that the way a particular age depicted Jesus is an essential key to

understanding that age. The later chapters of the book show that "as respect for the organized church has declined, reverence for Jesus has grown."

4. Robert Farrar Capon, *Between Noon and Three* (San Francisco: Harper & Row, 1982), pp. 114-15, quoted in Donald W. McCullough, *Waking from the American Dream* (Downers Grove, Ill.: InterVarsitv Press, 1988).

5. De Mello, pp. 113-14.

6. Marcus S. Borg, *Jesus, A New Vision, Spirit, Culture and the Life of Discipleship* (New York: Harper & Row, 1987), p. 35.

7. Paul Tillich, *The Shaking of the Foundations* (New York: Scribner's, 1948), pp. 161-62.

8. Hans Küng, *On Being a Christian* (New York: Doubleday, 1976), pp. 507-08. Kung is one of those rare thinkers incapable of superficial thought. I find it difficult to state the value and importance of this book in my life without hyperbole.

Chapter 2

1. This fascinating collection of scientific data was drawn from a Rotary Club presentation in Sea Island, Georgia in 1978. The speaker's name is not available to me at this time.

2. Peter Van Breemen, *Certain As the Dawn* (Denville, N.J.: Dimension Books, 1980), p. 13.

3. Walter J. Burghardt, S.J., *Grace on Crutches: Homilies for Fellow Travelers* (New York: Paulist Press, 1985), pp. 101-02.

4. Ibid., p. 108.

5. Flannery O'Connor, *The Complete Stories* (New York: Farrar, Straus and Giroux, 1971), p. 491. The author (1925-64) died of incurable lupus and left behind a body of fiction, especially short stories, that rank as Christian classics. Before her death she said, "You will have found Christ when you are concerned with other people's sufferings and not your own."

6. Gerhard Ebeling, *Luther, An Introduction to His Thought* (Philadelphia: Fortress Press, 1970), pp. 45-46.

7. Jeff Stone et al., *Growing Up Catholic* (New York: Doubleday, 1984), pp. 15-16.

8. Van Breemen, p. 61.

Chapter 3

1. Donald P. Gray, *Jesus, the Way to Freedom* (Winona, Minn.: St. Mary's College, 1979), p. 38. This little seventy-two-page jewel is scholarly yet eminently readable. It breathes the air of the gospel of grace. Gray's vision of Jesus is like refreshing rain falling on parched earth. Highly recommended.

2. Simon Tugwell, *The Beatitudes: Soundings in Christian Traditions* (Springfield, Ill.: Templegate Publishers, 1980), p. 7. In my opinion, of the scores of books written on the Beatitudes, none have matched the depth and wisdom of Tugwell's book.

3. Albert Nolan, *Jesus before Christianity* (Maryknoll, N.Y.: Orbis Books, 1978), p. 56. Nolan presents a portrait of Jesus before he became enshrined in doctrines, dogma, and ritual. A valuable and compelling little work.

4. Ibid., p. 23.

5. Brennan Manning, *A Stranger to Self-hatred* (Denville, N.J.: Dimension Books, 1983), p. 47.

6. Nolan, p. 39.

7. Nolan, p. 56.

8. Edward Schillebeeckx, *Jesus: An Experiment in Christology* (New York: Scabury Press, 1976), p. 165.

9. Walter Kasper, *Jesus the Christ* (New York: Paulist Press, 1977), p. 86. I found the author's prose heavy and the style ingratiating, but a careful reading reaps rich rewards.

10. Robert C. Frost, *Our Heavenly Father* (Plainfield, N.J.: Logos International, 1978), p. 44. Frost credibly and imaginatively reconstructs the hidden life of Jesus before He began His public ministry. Recommended for Bible study and small group discussion.

11. Burghardt, p. 144.

12. Gerald S. Sloyan, *Jesus in Focus: A Life in Its Setting* (Mystic, Conn.: Twenty-Third Publications, 1986), p. 38.

Chapter 4

1. De Mello, pp. 114-15.

2. Gray, p. 33.

3. Ibid., p. 19.

4. Eugene Kennedy, *The Choice to be Human* (New York: Doubleday, 1985), p. 128.

5. Donald W. McCullough, *Waking From the American Dream* (Downers Grove, Ill.: InterVarsity Press, 1988), p. 116. The spirit of his book permeates

the pages of mine, especially his chapter "The Difference Friday Makes." I am indebted to Dr. McCullough and understand why Richard Halverson, the chaplain of the U.S. Senate, wrote: "This book is imperative reading for all who take Christ seriously."

6. Peter Van Breemen, *As Bread That Is Broken*, (Denville, N.J.: Dimension Books, 1975), p. 196.

7. Gerald G. May, *Addiction and Grace* (San Francisco: Harper & Row, 1988), p. 166. This book broadens our understanding of addiction (which can range from cocaine to an idea) and the gentle interplay of grace in regaining our freedom.

8. De Mello, p. 74.

Chapter 5

1. Joan Puls, *A Spirituality of Compassion* (Mystic, Conn.: Twenty-Third Publications, 1988), pp. 119-20.

2. Sean Caulfield, *The God of Ordinary People* (Kansas City, Mo.: Sheed and Ward, 1988), p. 50.

3. Puls, p. 120.

4. James N. McCutcheon, "The Righteous and the Good," in *Best Sermons* (San Francisco: Harper & Row, 1988), pp. 238-39.

5. Frederick Buechner, *The Magnificent Defeat* (San Francisco: Harper & Row, 1985), p. 47.

6. Andrew M. Greeley, *God in Popular Culture* (Chicago, Ill.: The Thomas More Press, 1988), p. 124.

7. Peter S. Hawkins, *The Language of Grace* (Cambridge, Mass.: Cowley Publications, 1983), pp. 67-68. The author examines the fiction of Flannery

O'Connor, Walker Percy, and Irish Murdock and examines the language of grace they employ to confront the modern reader on the premise that many of the traditional words on grace have been devalued.

8. Walter J. Burghardt, *Still Proclaiming Your Wonders* (New York: Paulist Press, 1984), p. 170.

9. Brennan Manning, *Prophets and Lovers* (Denville, N.J.: Dimension Books, 1976), pp. 12-14. Here I have condensed a broad biblical theology of divine agape in one of my previously published works.

Chapter 6

1. Richard Selzer, M.D., *Mortal Lessons: Notes on the Art of Surgery* (New York: Simon and Shuster, 1978), pp. 45-46. I first read this story in *The Wittenburg Door*, an often satirical Christian magazine that advertises itself as "the perfect gift for the closed mind." I always await the next issue with considerable anticipation.

2. Jurgen Moltmann, *The Crucified God* (New York: Harper & Row, 1974), p. 108.

3. Joachim Jeremias, *The Parables of Jesus* (New York: Charles Scribner's, Sons, 1970) p. 72.

4. Ibid., p. 188.

5. Tugwell, p. 23.

6. John Shea, *Stories of God* (Chicago, Ill.: Thomas More Press, 1978), p. 187. One of the most original and creative thinkers in the American church today.

7. McCullough, p. 122.

8. John R. Claypool, "Learning to Forgive Ourselves," in *Best Sermons 1* (San Francisco: Harper & Row, 1988), p. 269.

9. Quote from St. Francis de Sales. Source unknown.

10. Walter J. Burghardt, *Tell the Next Generation* (New York: Paulist Press, 1980), p. 43.

11. Jon Sobrino, *Christology at the Crossroads, A Latin American Approach* (Maryknoll, N.Y.: Orbis Books, 1978), p. 171.

12. Burghardt, *Grace on Crutches*, p. 43.

Chapter 7

1. I have developed this true account in a different fashion in my "Gentle Revolutionaries."

2. Dietrich Bonhoeffer, *Life Together* (San Francisco: Harper & Row, 1954), quoted in Bob and Michael Benson, *Disciplines For the Inner Life* (Waco, Tex.: Word Books, 1985), p. 60. A helpful little book of guided Scripture readings coupled with the writings of spiritual leaders in order to deepen the inner life.

3. C.S. Lewis, *The Problem of Pain* (New York: Macmillan), pp. 49-50.

4. Anthony De Mello, *The Song of the Bird* (Anand, India: Gujaret Sahitya Prakash, distributed by Chicago, Ill.: Loyola University Press, 1983), p. 130.

5. Kennedy, pp. 8-9. Kennedy's book, subtitled *Jesus Alive in the Gospel of Matthew*, ranks in the top ten of the best books I have read in the past ten years.

6. Brennan Manning, *The Wisdom of Accepted*

Tenderness (Denville, N.J.: Dimension books, 1978), p. 55.

7. May, p. 169.

Chapter 8

1. Hans Küng, *Freedom Today* (New York: Sheed and Ward, 1966), pp. 36-37. The passage from *Brothers Karamazov* was cited here.

2. Brother Roger, *Parable of Community* (Minneapolis, Minn.: Seabury Press, 1980), p. 4.

3. Henri J. M. Nouwen, *Lifesigns, Intimacy, Fecundity, and Ecstasy in Christian Perspective* (New York: Doubleday, 1986), p. 38. A fine little book offering the essential key to a life free from the domination of fear.

4. Gray, p. 45.

5. William Kilpatrick, *Identity and Intimacy* (New York: Sheed and Ward, 1975), p. 112.

6. Carl J. Jung, *Modern Man in Search of a Soul* (Harcourt, Brace and World Harvest Books, 1933), p. 235.

7. M. Basil Pennington, *Centering Prayer: Renewing an Ancient Christian Prayer Form* (Garden City, N.Y.: Doubleday, 1980), pp. 68-69. The great value of this book lies in the simplicity and clarity of the presentation. A way of praying that leads to a deep, living relationship with God.

8. Anthony De Mello, *The Heart of the Enlightened* (New York: Doubleday, 1989), p. 122.

9. John L. McKenzie, *Source: What the Bible Says*

about the Problems of Contemporary Life (Chicago: Thomas More Press, 1984), p. 146.

10. Küng, *Freedom Today.*

11. Fyodor Dostoyevsky, *The Brothers Karamozov* (New York: Modern Library, Random House, 1934), p. 272. One of the most enduring masterpieces ever written with the opening inscription, "I tell you most solemnly, unless a grain of wheat falls on the ground and dies, it remains only a single grain; but if it dies, it yields a rich harvest" (John 12:24).

Chapter 9

1. Gerald O'Collins, *The Second Journey, Spiritual Awareness and the Mid-Life Crisis* (New York: Paulist Press, 1978), p. 4.

2. Ibid., p. 62. This book offers a compassionate insight into the anxiety and inner turmoil that often accompanies the crisis of the middle years. It is encouraging to read the stories of others who have walked this well-trod path.

3. Brennan Manning, *Souvenirs of Solitude* (Denville, N.J.: Dimension Books, 1979), pp. 8-28. Here I drew material from a previous work of mine now out of print.

Chapter 10

1. Russell Baker, *Growing Up* (New York: Signet Books, New American Library, 1982), pp. 259-60.

2. Lloyd Ogilvie, *Ask Him Anything* (Waco, Tex.: Word Books, 1981), quoted in Bob and Michael W. Benson, *Disciplines for the Inner Life* (Waco, Tex.: Word Books, 1985).

3. Victor Rangel-Ribeiro, *Reader's Digest*, August 1989, p. 76.

4. Puls, p. 119.

5. Annie Dillard, *Pilgrim at Tinker Creek* (New York: Harper's Magazine Press, 1974), p. 276.

6. Louis Evely, *That Man Is You* (New York: Paulist Press, 1964), p. 121.

7. Henri J. M. Nouwen, "The Prodigal Comes Home," *National Catholic Reporter*, 4 August 1989.

8. Robert Bolt, *A Man for All Seasons* (New York: Random House, 1960), p. 140.

9. G.K. Chesterton, *The Fame of Blessed Thomas More* (New York: Sheed and Ward, 1929), p. 63.

Chapter 11

1. This insight and story of the visit with the Amish family has provided me with a new perception of the 'born again' experience. A previous work of mine, *The Signature of Jesus*, contains this account.

2. May, p. 192.

3. Andrew Greeley, *What a Modern Catholic Believes About God* (Chicago: Thomas More Press, 1971), p. 91-92. Prior to Greeley's career as a novelist, he wrote two books on the theology of the Old and New Testament and revealed a remarkable gift for synthesis.

4. Louis M. Savary & Patricia H. Berne, *Prayerways* (San Francisco: Harper & Row, 1980), p. 7.

5. De Mello, *The Song of the Bird*, p. 39.

A Word After

1. Eugene Peterson, *Traveling Light* (Downers Grove, Ill.: InterVarsity Press, 1982), p. 39.